MW00827728

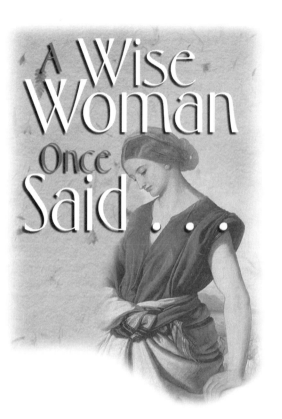

A Wise Woman Once Said . . .

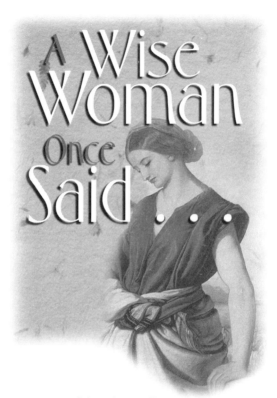

A Wise Woman Once Said

Shirley Rose

Bridge-Logos

Gainesville, Florida 32614 USA

A WISE WOMAN ONCE SAID...
by Shirley Rose

Bridge-Logos *Publishers*
P.O. Box 141630
Gainesville, FL 32614
www.bridgelogos.com

International Standard Book Number: 0-88270-8899

Unless noted as TLB, all scripture quotations are from
the New King James Version of the Bible, Copyright
1982, Thomas Nelson Inc. Used by Permission. All
rights reserved. Scripture quotations noted TLB are from
The Living Bible edition identified as Copyright 1971.
Used by permission of Tyndale House Publishers. All
rights reserved.

Dedication

*T*his book is dedicated to all the wise and beautiful women in my life who have helped me to become who I am today. Some of them are no longer with us, but their powerful influence lives on in me and in the many other lives they touched.

Vanessa Bogdan
My daughter

Tara Duncan
My niece

Margaret Ewing
My Chicago mom

Geraldene Rider
My mother

Esther Ringe
My sister

Emily Rose
My daughter-in-law

Jackie Rose
My mother-in-law

Rentia Rose
My daughter-in-law

Myrtle Smith
My aunt

Acknowledgements

My heartfelt thanks go to Professor Jeffrey Rose, my brilliant son, whose scholarship and grasp of the Old Testament have added so much richness to this book. Jeff, it has been a joy to learn from you, and your encouragement has been priceless.

Also, to my excellent producer Nancy Hanna, who thought of this title in two seconds flat. Your creativity never ceases to amaze me.

Contents

Introduction

She is more precious than rubies...
Her ways are ways of pleasantness,
And all her paths are peace.
She is a tree of life
to those who take hold of her,
And happy are all who retain her.

*W*ho do these beautiful verses describe? If you read Proverbs 3:13-18 you will discover these verses were written about wisdom, one of the most desirable virtues anyone can possess. The diverse meanings of "wisdom" include intelligence, perception, understanding, good judgment, insight, knowledge, and skill.

It is interesting to note in the verses above that wisdom is given the feminine gender. Throughout Jewish and Christian history wisdom is often described as a woman. The roots of this idea can be found in the Psalms, in Hebrew poetry, and in Wisdom of Sirah, which is one of the books of the Apocrypha.

The Apocrypha is still retained in the Roman Catholic Bible although it has not been included in the Protestant Bible since Martin Luther. But these writings, nonetheless, provide yet another insight into the theme that runs throughout the old and new testaments and that has continued to shape Christian values through the ages; wisdom is beautiful, holy, and decidedly womanly.

Unfortunately, women today are bombarded with convoluted family roles, smutty magazines, immoral films and television programs, and a choice of lifestyles that glorify selfishness.

To find the role models we need to live and grow in the ways the Lord intends, let's look for a moment to the women of the Bible. These women are among the most provocative and fascinating women in history. There was nothing dull about their lives. They were women of passion, triumph, influence, and genuine wisdom. And they used their God-given gifts to make a difference for good, and, in many cases, that difference continued to unfold in important ways for many, many generations.

Let's consider the strengths as well as the weaknesses and vulnerabilities of these legendary women. As we do, you may be surprised to discover that these women were not so different from you and me. It is even more surprising to realize that we can be like them.

It is my sincere hope that the simple, step-by-step suggestions in this book will empower you to become more and more like the wise women of the Bible.

Let's listen now to what they have to say to us…and learn from them.

Abigail
Peacemaker

David said to Abigail,
"Praise be to the Lord, the God of Israel,
who has sent you today to meet me.

May you be blessed
for your good judgement . . . "

1 Samuel 25:32-33

Abigail
Peacemaker

My name is Abigail. The night is growing closer now. This little donkey knows the path well, but I must urge him forward at a pace he does not like. He flicks his ears at me as if to say, "What is the great hurry?" But there is not a moment to lose.

Most people would consider me fortunate. My husband owns a successful business, and we are very rich. We have many servants, plenty of food, and thousands of sheep and goats. But there is no joy in any of it. How often I have heard other women speak with envy about the life that my husband and I lead. If they only knew the truth.

My husband Nabal is selfish and cruel; I cannot respect him no matter how hard I try.

His name means "fool," and he lives down to that name far too often. He is drunk most of the time. He's crude and boorish and evil in all his dealings with other people. He ignores the children, which is probably a blessing. Even our servants don't respect him. His tongue is always getting him into trouble. I have tried far too many times over the years to smooth things over with our neighbors. But this time he's gone too far.

He has insulted David, God's anointed one, although David and his men have done nothing wrong. Instead, they assisted Nabal's shepherds when they were grazing our sheep in the wilderness. David's men were honorable and kind and took not one lamb for their own use. David's soldiers offered our shepherds protection from the thieves that are so common in that wilderness.

But what thanks does Nabal give for their kindness? When they came to our home seeking hospitality on a feast day, Nabal pretended not to know who David was. (Oh, he knows who he is all right. Nabal has been a stubborn supporter of Saul even though Nabal is well aware of Saul's treachery.) My husband refused to give David's good men even meager provisions. He insulted them openly and put our whole family in danger.

When one of our servants told me how my husband had mistreated David's men, I had to act quickly. I have already sent the servants on ahead with the donkeys loaded with gifts of food and wine to meet David's approaching army. I can only hope the meat and raisins, bread, and figs will help to cool David's anger. Now I must go myself and meet him face to face and try to reason with him. I pray I can reach him before he and his four hundred armed soldiers reach us. I should see the dust from his horses just over this hill.

I would rather be anywhere on earth than here tonight. But I must cover for my husband yet one more time and try to undo the mess he's made of things.

"Oh, God of my fathers, help me. Use me to bring peace. Let me find favor in David's sight. Let him show mercy to my family and to me. Please, don't let me be too late."

(Narrative based on I Samuel 25)

Abigail's Answers for Today

My heart is saddened as I read about this extraordinary woman of the Old Testament. The Bible tells us that Abigail was beautiful and intelligent. While many Bible women are called "beautiful," this is the only time outward appearance is so blatantly coupled with an even greater asset, an astute mind. Despite such assets, however, Abigail's situation was tragic. Her husband Nabal was boorish, crude, ignorant, and a "son of Belial," which means he was not a believer. He did not serve Abigail's God. He was also a supporter of Saul; therefore, he shared the rejected king's jealousy of David.

What a mismatched pair! Abigail was poised, possessing good judgment, smart, beautiful, charming and respected by the community and her own servants. Her religious witness and her knowledge of Jewish history indicate that she had a background of godly training and was acquainted with the teachings of the prophets. Her approach to David shows that she was very much aware of the politics and events in her own world. [1]

You may wonder why a lovely person like Abigail would throw her life away by marrying someone like Nabal. It was, however, the custom of those times for marriages to be arranged by men. The women had very little to say about it. Since Nabal was from a wealthy family and had considerable wealth, he was probably considered a good catch for Abigail. But her troubled marriage proved the opposite. One lesson to be learned from this story is the inevitable heartache that comes with being unequally yoked with an unbeliever.

Abigail is like many women I meet today. Like Abigail, they cannot respect their husbands no matter how hard they try. They are married to cruel, insensitive, and often abusive men. These women are not only hurting, but continually find themselves in a position of having to cover for their husbands. They are faced perhaps daily with a decision.

Do they get angry and return evil for evil? Do they remain neutral and bury their heads thinking he will eventually get what he deserves? Or do they act as peacemaker?

Abigail chose to act as a peacemaker, and she used every ounce of creativity and resourcefulness she could muster to salvage an otherwise disastrous situation.

In so many households today, strife, not peace, is standard. I believe the wife and mother sets the emotional tone for the household regardless of the challenges she faces. There are many scriptures dealing with the subject of strife. It is clear that creating strife is considered a sin. In fact, in Galatians 5:19 and 20, Paul lists the works of the flesh, all the sins that would prevent us from inheriting the kingdom of God. There are some pretty grave offenses listed there, such as idolatry, murder, adultery, and sorcery. But right in the middle of these horrible sins are "hatred, contentions, jealousies, wrath, and dissensions." How sobering a thought that a sin like creating strife or contention is looked upon with the same seriousness as adultery or murder!

The Bible has a surprising number of verses dealing with strife as it relates to husbands and wives. Consider the following:

> *Better is a dry morsel with quietness,*
> *than a house full of feasting with strife.*
> Proverbs 17:1 NKJV

A home filled with strife and division destroys itself.

Mark 3:25 TLB

A foolish son is the ruin of this father, and the contentions of a wife are a continual dripping.

Proverbs 19:13 NKJV

I believe that, in any situation, we can make a choice to create peace instead of strife.

Abigail made the more difficult choice. She determined, with God's help, to undo the damage Nabal had done. She knew that her very life and the lives of her children were at stake. She decided to take gifts of food and provision to David and his men. She would humble herself and intercede on behalf of her husband and her household.

As Abigail directed the loading of the food onto the donkeys, she probably recited over and over in her head the speech she would make when she saw David. How she must have trembled just thinking of facing this powerful man! He was a legend. His successful military campaigns were unequaled. He was the topic of conversation in every household, in every city. He would soon be King of Israel.

Abigail may have been happy to meet David someday, face-to-face. But not like this. The very thought of meeting with him must have filled her with terror. But she never hesitated. She sent the gifts on ahead to David, then she followed.

Abigail boldly intercepted this powerful leader who was bent on vengeance for Nabal's insults and parsimony. As Abigail dismounted her donkey and bowed low before David, her amazing words present the perfect profile of a peacemaker. Consider and imitate her wise and effective strategy.

Profile of a Peacemaker
Be willing to accept the blame

I accept all blame in this matter, my lord.
Please listen to what I want to say.
Nabal is a bad-tempered boor, but please
don't pay any attention to what he said.
He is a fool—just like his name means.
But I didn't see the messengers you sent.
And now, here is a present I have brought
to you and your young men.

I Samuel 25:24,25 TLB

*W*ow! What a lesson in peacemaking! The first words out of Abigail's mouth were an admission of guilt. This was certainly a demonstration of her great wisdom. Before she said anything else, she took the blame.

How we fight to be right! I am reminded with shame how, even during a simple disagreement with my husband, I strive to win the argument, instead of trying to make peace. I rationalize my actions. I defend my wrongdoings as though my very life depends on it. I bring up all the past sins and failures of my husband, all in a desperate struggle to win!

If we could only learn, the fastest and surest way to neutralize a volatile situation is to take the blame. It disarms. It takes the fight right out of the person who might be our opponent. Assuming the blame is the best way to make peace.

Did Abigail really feel responsible for what had happened? No! She even goes on to admit she didn't even see the messengers David sent. But she had already deflated David's anger by her willingness to take the blame.

Accepting blame is not an easy discipline. We are human; we all have the instinct of self-preservation. It is a natural defense mechanism to prove ourselves right and innocent. In addition, many of us carry the baggage of an injured ego or poor self-image. So the impulse and need to be right is even stronger. But the more we practice the peacemaking strategy of admission of guilt, the easier this practice becomes.

However, we must be convincing. We can sincerely and honestly accept blame because we are all, at one time or another, guilty. We are selfish by nature, and, if we are honest with ourselves, we can usually find a way we contributed to the problem.

Ask for and grant forgiveness.

Forgive my boldness in coming out here.
I Samuel 25:28a TLB

*I*f admission of guilt is difficult, asking for forgiveness is even harder. It is especially painful if we really do not believe ourselves to be the guilty party. The words, "I'm sorry; would you forgive me?" are some of the most difficult to utter. But there is always something we need forgiveness for. Abigail asked David to forgive her for her boldness in confronting him. And soon after, he granted her wish.

We must sincerely ask for forgiveness for our part in the problem. It doesn't count to say something like, "I'm sorry you are being such a jerk."

The strategy of asking for forgiveness, especially if we feel we are the injured one, is also a discipline perfected over time. We often resist asking for forgiveness because we don't want to admit guilt. For this reason, we are likely to find asking for forgiveness a lot easier once we have gotten past the issue of placing blame.

Even more important than asking for forgiveness is the willingness to be forgiving. We must learn to forgive quickly and completely when someone hurts us. This spiritual discipline not only makes us a peacemaker, it is absolutely essential for joy and physical well-being. Nothing is more unattractive than a bitter, grudge-holding attitude. (And bitterness is an attitude that will definitely show up on your face sooner or later.)

The noted Christian author Stormie Omartian, who has written about her abuse from her mother, such as being locked in a closet for hours at a time, says she was not able to receive healing from these scars and become whole again until she completely forgave her mother and made peace with her.

"Forgiveness does not make the other person right," Stormie writes. "But it does set you free."[2]

Find Something Positive to Say

The Lord will surely reward you
with eternal royalty for your descendants,
for you are fighting his battles;
and you will never do wrong
throughout your entire life.

I Samuel 25:28b TLB

*W*hen Abigail praised David, she demonstrated her wisdom as a peacemaker. Nothing is more effective in diffusing anger than a well-placed compliment. It would be interesting to know how many wars and catastrophes through history have been prevented by a word of encouragement or affirmation and how many have been caused by angry, careless words of criticism. One of the surest ways to make peace is to say something positive about the party or parties involved.

But the positive words must be the truth and stated sincerely if they are to be effective. Abigail was not just groveling because she knew her family was in danger. She was demonstrating to David her own humility and showing him respect by stating with sincerity what she expected God to do for him and his descendants. The surest way to any father's heart is through his children. Abigail's quick reference to David's descendants was intentional. She was reminding him that his actions that day would have lasting consequences.

Making and keeping peace in our homes and workplaces would be so much easier if we could grasp the concept of finding the positive in others rather than the negative. We are so tempted in many areas of life to focus on the negative. We so easily find fault in our husbands, children, bosses, and even pastors. I have often felt condemned, and rightfully so, after an evening out with my girlfriends when I realized we had amused ourselves by pointing out the faults and shortcomings of our husbands.

I have heard that for every criticism we give to a loved one, it takes four positive, affirming statements to neutralize the effects of the one negative comment. Yet we often fail to give our family members the positive reinforcement they need. Let us sincerely ask God to remind us of the importance of focusing on the positive. We need to look for uplifting, complimentary, and encouraging words with which to praise those around us.

Appeal to Reason and Common Sense

When the Lord has done all the good things
he promised you
and has made you king of Israel,
you won't want the conscience
of a murderer
who took the law into his own hands!

I Samuel 25:24-31 TLB

*F*inally, Abigail got practical. She appealed to David's common sense. She had worked her way through the steps of making peace to the point where David's anger had subsided, and he could think rationally. She realized that David, godly man that he was, would regret claiming vengeance and shedding blood. When she pointed out these facts to him, she prevented a great calamity.

We can appeal to common sense with someone only after his anger has subsided. When he is still emotional, defensive, and hurt, don't try to be rational or appeal to any noble qualities or sense of purpose. It simply won't work. But once the ego is intact and the emotions are calm, then a logical solution and course of action can be discussed.

This is also a good opportunity to work out a plan for improvement so that the same problem will not continue to occur over and over again, creating strife unnecessarily. At such a time, you can work out a compromise, or, at the very least, point out, as Abigail did, the consequences of the angry actions.

A few years ago, I had to do some pretty radical compromising when it came to my husband Jerry's shoes and socks lying around the house. For some time, there had been a lot of strife in our home over this issue. I became so irritated over it that I would throw his shoes and socks into the basement or garage. I threatened to put his dirty socks into his pillowcase. But nothing I tried changed his habit. And I exerted so much effort trying to change his behavior that I was exhausting myself. I finally realized it took much less energy to pick up after him. So I simply decided to pick up his shoes and socks and carry them to a less-obtrusive location. (I am still not spiritual enough to put them in his closet where they belong.)

Now, every couple of weeks, when the pile gets ridiculous, and I can no longer walk in my laundry room, I ask Jerry to put them away. And he does so very agreeably. I am not nagging him all the time, and he seems to appreciate my new approach. It was incredibly freeing for me when I decided I would no longer allow this issue to create strife and arguments in my home!

Obviously, couples face much more serious disputes than dirty socks lying around the house. But often such petty issues can create an undercurrent of strife in homelife.

In the case of David and Abigail, he was grateful for her intervention in his plan that day. She prevented him from doing something he may have regretted for the rest of his life. In verses 32-34, David says:

…Bless the Lord God of Israel who has sent you to meet me today!

Thank God for your good sense!

Bless you for keeping me from murdering the man and carrying out vengeance with my own hands.

A woman who creates peace out of strife is always appreciated and worthy of admiration and praise. And she is always rewarded.

Rewards of a Peacemaker

The ministry of being a peacemaker is one of the most rewarding. Abigail was rewarded for her intervention in David's life in a most astounding way. Let's take a look at the conclusion of her story.

After David accepted her gifts and assured her of her family's safety, she returned home. Nabal had given a huge party and was roaring drunk (no great surprise there). (I Samuel 25: 36) In his drunken ignorance, Nabal was totally oblivious to the danger he was in and unaware of how his wife had just saved his life. And Abigail, again wisely choosing her timing, did not tell him what had happened that night. She waited until the next morning when he was sober.

Then, when he heard about his close call with a disaster that he had caused, he had what was probably a stroke. He was paralyzed for about ten days and then died. The scripture says, "The Lord killed him."

There was no grief on David's part when he heard about Nabal's death. David says in Verse 39,

*Praise the Lord! God has paid back Nabal
and kept me from doing it myself; he has
received his punishment for his sin.*

David let no grass grow under his feet. He immediately asked Abigail to be his wife, and she consented. She had obviously made quite an impression that night as she met him in the field. And why wouldn't she? He was impressed not only by her physical beauty, but also by her intelligence, humility, and wisdom.

I don't mean to imply that if we become a peacemaker, God will reward us by taking an undesirable husband out of the picture or that we will receive a marriage proposal from a handsome king. That sounds more like a fairy tale than real life, doesn't it? However, this true story from the Bible does demonstrate that there are always blessings connected with being a peacemaker.

Whenever and however you can create peace, someone will always be grateful. Whether it is you who is personally involved in the conflict, or if you are acting as a moderating third party, the benefits are the same. By making peace, you will always do unspeakable good.

The effects of your ministry of peace will be far-reaching beyond your wildest dreams. You can prevent irreparable harm. At the very least you will avert harsh words that could damage a person's spirit forever.

Words spoken in anger can never be recalled. They can be forgiven and forgotten, with God's help, but too often the scars are permanent. As Robert Burton has said, "A blow with a word strikes deeper than a blow with a sword."[3]

Abigail demonstrated some amazing wisdom that we can admire and imitate. She proved she had brains as well as beauty. She made the best of her difficult circumstances. She took the initiative; she was proactive. She was generous and creative. She showed unusual resourcefulness. She was willing to take risks. In all these ways, Abigail created peace instead of strife. She was a beautiful peacemaker.

If we do everything we can to be a fixer, to salvage potentially tragic situations, to make peace out of chaos, we will always win. We can with confidence leave the outcome to the Lord, knowing He is truly the Prince of Peace.

End Notes

1 Herbert Lockyer, *All the Women of the Bible*, (Zondervan,) p. 23

2 Stormie Omartian, *Stormie: A Story of Forgiveness and Healing* (Harvest House Publishers, September, 1977).

3 Burton Stevenson, *The Home Book of Quotations* (Crown Publishers, Inc., New York), p. 2224

Study Guide

More to Explore

Abigail was one of the most intelligent women in the Bible. Her story takes us through the often-difficult, yet brilliant steps to creating peace. She turned a potential disaster into a wonderful future when she made peace and cleared the path for God's will.

Read the following verses to expand your study of peacemaking and answer the accompanying questions.

- Matthew 10:16
- Matthew 5:9
- James 3:17, 18
- Ephesians 4:3
- Hebrews 12:14

Consider this . .

Is the atmosphere in your home one of peace
or strife? Explain.

_____

_____

List three things you have said or done this
week that may have created strife between you
and another person.

_____

What was the result of your words and
actions?

_____

_____

What are some strife-filled situations in your
family or workplace that you might change
through being a peacemaker?

_____

_____

_____

List several opportunities you had this week to make peace.

_____

_____

Why did you choose to either ignore or embrace them?

_____

_____

What were the results?

_____

Are you guilty of finding fault and focusing on the negative more often than the positive?

_____

Write down some compliments for each family member and deliver them throughout the week. Watch for the surprising results!

_____

_____

Wise Reflections

The word "peacemaker" is a compound word, two words combined into one. Therefore, to be peacemakers, we must be willing to "make peace"—sometimes even from extreme hatred or anger!

As in anything else that is made, there are ingredients that go into making peace, too. Abigail provided us the perfect recipe for peace. Her noble components include wisdom, humility, forgiveness, courage, gentleness and restraint.

Consider any strife, contention, or frustration you are experiencing today. Briefly write a recipe for your own peace plan. List your ingredients (such as patience, perseverance, compassion), and then explain how you'll combine them to produce the peace God desires you to have in your life.

Esther
Heroine

*"I will go in to see the king;
and if I perish, I perish."*

Esther 4:16

Esther
Heroine

My Hebrew name is Hadassah. But here in Persia, I'm known as Esther, which means star. More than a year ago, my cousin Mordecai brought me to the palace of King Ahasuerus. Though many other virgins surrounded me there, the king favored me above them all and chose me to be his queen.

The king also has many concubines, and it's been a month since he last called for me. Now I'm waiting to see if he will give me an audience. I've never been more terrified in my life!

When Mordecai brought me to the palace, I knew my life was taking an amazing turn. During the entire time of preparation leading up to my first meeting with the king, part of me felt that I was totally out of place. What was I, a Hebrew orphan girl, doing here with the most beautiful and sophisticated maidens from all over Persia? What did I know of the expensive oils, perfumes, and beauty treatments I was given for a whole year? I had lived a simple life with Mordecai, who has been like a father to me.

Yet, despite the stange surroundings of the palace, another part of me felt at peace—as if this unexpected turn of events was part of my destiny. I felt in some odd way that I did belong here.

Now I wear the queen's crown upon my head. I still can hardly believe and accept it. But it is becoming clear to me why I was chosen to replace Queen Vashti, who disobeyed the king.

Perhaps it was for this very night that I came to the palace. It could be for this very reason that I was born. Yet, it could also be the last night of my life.

The king has always been kind to me, and I believe he loves me in his own way—as much as he is capable of loving. But he still frightens me, even in our most intimate moments. He is, after all, the king—the most powerful man in the world. And he is well aware of his power.

Would he be as gentle and considerate with me if he knew I was a Hebrew? Would his smile be as warm? Or would his love turn to hatred? I have seen his wrath burn against his enemies, and it is terrifying.

I would do anything for my cousin Mordecai, but this plan he's devised is so dangerous. I'm not even sure it will work. What will I say to Ahasuerus? On the other hand, what choice do I have? If I do not attempt to speak to the king tonight, the Jewish people – my people – will be slaughtered. There's no way of knowing how this night will end, but I know everything will be different from now on. Everything will change.

The time is close now. I must walk through that door and face the king. If he does not raise his scepter to accept my visit, I will be put to death for approaching his throne unbidden. And even if he does raise the scepter to me, I must reveal to him my Jewish heritage and ask him to revoke one of his laws.

Perhaps I will receive his favor once more. Perhaps he will grant my request. I must try. It is the only chance I have of saving my people.

I will go to the king. And if I perish as a result, so be it.

(Narrative based on Esther 1-10.)

Esther's Answers for Today

*O*ne of the most amazing things about the book of Esther is that God is not mentioned once. Yet Esther's story is a dramatic portrayal of God's hidden hand at work in His people's lives and destinies. God demonstrates His care and protection, which is also available to us today. It is the story of a truly beautiful woman, a spunky orphan whom God thrust into greatness for a strategic moment in history.

Esther is one of the few women of the Bible whose outward beauty is addressed in such a straightforward way. Her outward beauty was put to the test long before her inner qualities were. Her story is a graphic demonstration of how outward beauty is also a gift of God, and how it can be used as a tool in His hand for the noblest of purposes. Here's how it happened.

It all started with a beauty contest. This was no ordinary beauty pageant. The stakes were very high. The competition was incredibly difficult. And the prize surpassed anything ever offered before. The winner would be crowned queen of Persia. She would replace Queen Vashti, now fallen from grace since disregarding the king's order to appear in public.

King Xerxes (Ahasuerus) was the most powerful monarch up to his time. He ruled over half the known world.

Queen Vashti, his wife, was not a woman of royal blood who ruled next to her husband as we see in later cultures. She was "queen" of the harem—the reigning favorite wife at the time. This "chief wife" or "queen consort" was privileged to wear the royal tiara and was the acknowledged head of the female apartments. The other concubines honored her by actual prostration. Queen Vashti had great wealth of her own, not necessarily by the will of the king, but by established law. The Persian queen dressed in splendid attire and the extravagant ornamentation can only be imagined.[1]

But even with lavish surroundings and jewelry, being queen of the harem doesn't sound like a picnic to me. Can you imagine being one of many, perhaps hundreds of wives? Talk about competition and jealousy! And once these wives were chosen, they were essentially prisoners for life.

Eunuchs (castrated men) attended the harem and provided communication between the king and his wives. These eunuchs, also known as chamberlains, often became close advisors of the king and could attain great political power.[2] They were highly trusted because they had no wives or children to divide their loyalty or distract them from their occupation.

Unfortunately, these eunuchs were the only men the king's wives ever saw aside from the king. These poor women were isolated from society and might be summoned to the king only once! The whole setup suggests an exaggerated sense of power of the king contrasted with the lowly status of women. In the king's harem, beautiful young women existed merely for his pleasure and amusement.

It became obvious, however, that Queen Vashti was no milk toast. After a huge seven-day party given by the king, he had called for the queen to show off her beauty. This was a huge breach of etiquette because in Persia, unlike Babylon, the women had their own feasts and did not join the men.[3]

Vashti was not just being arbitrary when she refused his request. Her status demanded more respect than this. On the other hand, no one dared stand up to the king. But this number-one wife refused to be a spectacle for his drunken friends.

The king was furious and called his advisors together to discuss what was to be done. Apparently, this had never happened before. The advisors were afraid that if word got out, all the "noble ladies" of Persia would despise their husbands and also refuse to obey. Queen Vashti, the first liberated woman, had them all running scared. So the king's advisors convinced the king to punish Queen Vashti by finding a replacement.

The stage was now set for the beauty contest. Young virgins were gathered from every province to compete for Vashti's former post as queen of the harem. Esther, a lovely young Jewish girl, a foreigner, entered the picture as one of the candidates.

Esther did not resist the beauty treatments required for an entire year before seeing the king. But when the time came, she demonstrated modesty and good judgment. Having been offered all the "bells and whistles" the wealth of Persia could provide, she chose only the basics. The Bible says she "refused all but what was suggested by the attendant" (Esther 2:15).

Many of us women—including myself— tend to think more is better. If a little make-up, jewelry, etc. is good, a lot is better. Those of us who have an outgoing, sanguine personality tend to dress flamboyantly and have a tendency to overdo it. We need to rediscover the beautiful virtues of moderation and modesty, which equal good taste and even godliness.

When it was Esther's turn to go to the king, he favored her above all the other virgins. In fact, we are told that the king loved Esther more than the other women, and he crowned her queen. She must have been an extraordinary beauty.

The next character to appear in this drama is the villain, Haman, who felt that Esther's cousin and guardian, Mordecai, had failed to give him proper respect. Haman harbored such an intense hatred toward Moredecai that it grew into a vendetta. And this vendetta was not against Mordecai alone—but against all

Jewish people. Is this not typical of the illogical and tragic roots of most prejudice? Haman then convinced the king to decree that all the Jews in the land, every man, woman, and child should be killed.

This decree signaled the beginning of a long history of anti-Semitism and discrimination against the Jewish people. Haman was just one of several who had attempted the annihilation of the entire Hebrew race; you might consider him the Adolf Hitler of his day. However, God had His heroine in place. He had put her there "for such a time as this."

Esther's beauty and courage were both tested, and she passed with flying colors, providing a model for any of us who are asked to take a huge leap of faith to become God's heroine. Here are the requirements of genuine courage, a quality that often leads to greatness.

Profile of a Heroine
Overcome Your Fear

All the world knows that anyone,
whether man or woman,
who goes into the king's inner court
without his summons
is doomed to die
unless the king holds out his golden scepter;
Esther 4:10,11 TLB

*I*t is obvious from the Biblical account of Esther's story that she was very frightened about appealing to the king for her people. Besides, she had become rather comfortable in the "house of women." Why rock the boat?

More importantly, Esther knew the law. If she entered the king's presence without being called, she could be killed, and the king had not called for her in over a month. However, she overcame her fear when presented with an opportunity to stand in the gap for her whole nation; this was the most important decision of her life.

Have you ever been handed a once-in-a-lifetime opportunity to do something truly significant, but found yourself too timid, or unprepared, or downright terrified to try? Perhaps in your complacency you thought as Esther did, "Who am I to think I can pull this off?" Have you let your fear convince you to pass up an opportunity for greatness? Fear is common to all of us, but if we are to be true heroines for God, we must learn to overcome fear.

You may never be called upon to save a whole race of people. But chances are good that sooner or later God will ask you to do something radical—something that scares you or at the very least shoves you well out of your comfort zone.

"Radical" for one person might involve standing in front of a crowd and teaching. "Radical" for another could mean traveling to foreign lands and taking life-threatening risks.

Genuine courage says whatever the challenge, you will obey, in spite of your fear. It means being willing to act in obedience without any guarantees. Dark and frightening moments provide an opportunity for you to shine. It is in such moments that your true strength and inner beauty will show through.

Be Submissive and Obedient

*…though it is strictly forbidden, I will go
in to see the king and if I perish, I perish.*

Esther 4:16b

The Bible does not tell us whether the beautiful young virgins who were gathered from every surrounding province had a choice to go or not to go and vie for Vashti's crown. It merely says that Esther's cousin, Mordecai, brought her up to compete with the others.

Perhaps Mordecai was ordered to do so. Or perhaps he felt that since Esther was an orphan, it was the best chance she had for a successful future. Regardless of how it actually happened, Esther went willingly. She submitted to the year-long preparations and then later to the role of Xerxes' wife—queen of the harem.

This difficult role does not seem, at first glance, to be one that God would wish for his faithful servant Esther. And the situation has many features that would be distasteful to women. But the end of Esther's story reveals that she was exactly where God wanted her to be.

Have you ever found yourself in a situation that was more than you bargained for? You may feel, as Esther did, that part of you says this is wrong, out of place, and yet another part feels at peace, as though this is exactly where you belong. These are the times when submission and obedience are called for.

There are many aspects of obedience and submission. First, and most importantly, we should obey God's laws as spelled out in the Bible. We should seek to have such a close relationship with God that we can recognize His voice and learn to know his will. Submission to His will, then, is a natural outgrowth of our love and relationship with the Lord.

Women are to submit to their husbands as to the Lord, a subject many of us may not like but which is biblical nonetheless.

Another aspect of submission is how it relates to authority in general—an employer, a parent, a pastor, the law of the land. We cannot be truly beautiful women without the virtues of submission and obedience. Esther provides a great example of both qualities.

Seek Divine Guidance
and Help from Others

Go and gather together all the Jews
of Shushan and fast for me;
do not eat or drink for three days, night or
day; and I and my maids will do the same
Esther 4:16aTLB

*O*nce Esther made the decision to carry out
the dangerous yet imperative plan to save
her people, she realized she needed help. She
fasted and prayed and asked other Jews to do
likewise.

In a society that prides itself in its self-
sufficiency, we are often reluctant to ask for
help. We have been made to feel that for
women dependency is an ugly trait.
Remember that perfume commercial: "I can
bring home the bacon, fry it up in a pan. And
never, never let you forget you're a man.
'Cause I'm a woman, W-O-M-A-N."

The society we live in reminds us that if we
can't do it all, we are weak, unintelligent, or
inferior, but this is such a lie. If we could only
grasp the reality of the power released in us
when we become totally dependent on God for
his help and guidance. In fact, the surest way
to failure is to become self-sufficient.

When God asks you to step out into a risky situation, He will equip you to accomplish His task for you there. But He wants you to honestly admit your inadequacy for this task and rely on Him to accomplish it.

We must also be willing to ask for help and support from other believers. We should never be hesitant to ask others to pray for us. Likewise, we should request other types of help when we need it and be willing to freely give of ourselves as well.

Most of us fail to ask for help because of our pride. Whether it is a need for earnest prayer (even involving fasting), or financial help, or a gift of valuable time, we should be willing to ask. Then when God's will is accomplished through our lives, more of His people can share in the victory and blessing.

Wait for God's Timing

…If it please your Majesty,
I want you and Haman to come
to a banquet I have prepared for you today.
Esther 5:4

One of the most amazing aspects of Esther's story is the complicated plan she used to expose Haman and convince the king to change his own law. She knew that even after he extended the golden scepter to her, the most challenging and dangerous part of the plan was yet to be accomplished.

I'm sure that many of us would have been tempted to blurt out our request immediately. Esther, however, demonstrated patience and a sense of timing as she invited the king and Haman to a banquet and then, amazingly, to a second banquet the next day. With remarkable poise she carried out her plan.

Between the first and second banquet, the king discovered the service Mordecai had done for him and managed to reward him and unwittingly humiliate Haman at the same time.

The stage was set perfectly when Esther finally got around to asking the king to save her people (Esther 5-7).

We so often get impatient. We want things to happen in our time frame. We ask God for something and get angry with Him or give up hope when the answer is not immediately forthcoming. Our intentions may be to obey and act in accordance with God's will, but we often jump the gun or perhaps drag our feet and delay our obedience.

We expect God to do it all. Esther, on the other hand, prayed before formulating a plan of action. She had the patience and sense of timing to carry out that plan. It often takes more than just prayer to be God's woman of the hour. It may take planning, hard work, and sacrifice. And it always requires waiting for God's timing.

Rewards of Courage and Obedience

The obvious reward of Esther's courage **was** the salvation of all the Jews. She also received wealth and status. Her dear cousin, Mordecai, was highly exalted and honored not only in Shushan, but in all the provinces of the country. In this way she was able to repay his lifelong kindness to her.

Through Esther's actions and the response of the king, the position of the Jews changed radically throughout the land. They had once been ridiculed, ashamed of their heritage. Now they were honored and feared.

To commemorate the successful efforts of Esther and Mordecai, the annual celebration of Purim was established, so that future generations would never forget what had happened. "Pur" is a Persian word for "lots." It was called the feast of lots because the villain Haman actually resorted to casting lots to determine the best day to annihilate the Hebrew race. Jews of today still commemorate the holiday, Purim, by gathering at the synagogue, where the book of Esther is read. The celebration includes exuberant clapping of hands and stomping of feet to demonstrate contempt for Haman and joy for the deliverance of the Jews.[4]

Perhaps the greatest reward of our obedience to God's leading is the knowledge that we have contributed to the fulfillment of His vast plan. There is nothing more gratifying or faith-building than to look back over your life and see that your steps of faith landed you exactly where God wanted you, and that your being there helped further His kingdom.

It could have meant the establishment of a vital ministry, or the salvation of a lost soul, or the deliverance of a message of encouragement that changed a life forever. Or, as in Esther's case, it could mean the prevention of a great tragedy.

We must never underestimate the importance of being in God's will. Esther's is the best example I know of being in the right place at the right time.

Do you desire more courage? As faith grows, so does courage. The better we know God and His promises, the more we are willing to step out in faith to do his bidding.

No one becomes a great woman of faith overnight. It begins with taking baby steps and watching God's faithfulness, all the while trusting Him more and more. The Bible says faith comes by hearing, and hearing by the Word of God. Develop a love affair with God's word, and watch your faith and courage grow.

Esther demonstrated many other admirable characteristics: modesty, grace, confidence, and wisdom. In addition to her physical beauty, her great courage and patriotism is what she is remembered for. She was God's heroine because she overcame her fear and stepped outof her comfort zone.

I have found that as I strive to obey God, frightened as I may be, I receive the greatest reward of all—a sense of God's pleasure and approval. And I find as I walk through the door of the unknown, He always walks right beside me.

End Notes

1 James M. Freeman, *New Manners and Customs of the Bible*, Bridge-Logos, 1972, p. 204

2 Freeman, p. 203

3 Freeman, p. 203

4 Freeman, p. 207

Study Guide

More to Explore

*E*sther's courage, obedience and sense of timing resulted in the deliverance of her nation—God's chosen people. She was terribly afraid to step out of her comfort zone, even the dubious comfort of the king's harem. But Esther overcame her fear and faced the king.

Read the following Scripture verses to expand your study of courageous obedience, and then answer the accompanying questions.

- Joshua 1:6, 7
- 1 Corinthians 16:13, 14
- Proverbs 29:25
- 2 Timothy 1:7

Consider This . .

When has fear kept you from following God's leading?

What were your fears?

How does having strong, resilient faith help overcome fear and turn it to courage?

Has there been a time when you got ahead of God? Have you ever dragged behind? How can we flow better in God's timing?

List at least two instances when you trusted God as he called you out of your comfort zone and into action. How did it feel as your courage was strengthened along with your faith?

Wise Reflections . . .

Many people make the mistake of thinking beauty, brains, and self-confidence are synonymous with success. Esther, though a great beauty with obvious intelligence and personal strength, still relied on God and on her people for support as she sought to save the lives of an entire nation. Through Esther's remarkable example, we realize we can have the same reliance on God and his divine intervention if we are obedient to his plans.

Think for a moment about any fears, misgivings, or doubts you are experiencing. List your fears in the following areas of your life.

_____

Spiritual fear or doubt:

_____

Relationship-related fear and doubt:

_____

_____

Ministry or service-related fear or doubt:

_____

Work-related fear or doubt:

_____

_____

_____

Now pray that God will help you overcome these fears and through earnest prayer, fasting, and help and support from others.

Mary
Chosen One

I am the Lord's servant,
and I am willing to do
whatever he wants.
May everything you said come true.

Luke 1:38

Mary
Chosen One

My **journey is almost at an end**, and I will welcome the rest. The road up to these highlands has been steep, but the heat and this tedious, rocky climb have not diminished my happiness. My heart is so light that I have caught myself humming a melody more than once during this long trip, even though some might say I have nothing to sing about.

They might say I have disgraced my family and the kind, wonderful man who asked me to marry him. I can still see so vividly the hurt in Joseph's eyes and the disappointment and confusion on his dear face. I tried so hard to explain the visit from the angel, Gabriel. I could tell Joseph wanted to believe me. But how could he understand? I still don't understand it myself.

When I asked the angel how this could possibly happen, he said only that the Holy Spirit would visit me. Though I know that the miracle he told me about then has now occurred, it is still as much a mystery to me today as it was when the heavenly being appeared to me with his astonishing message. His news left me with a sense of peace and acceptance I have never known before. And I was surprised to hear myself saying, "Be it unto me." And I have, since that moment, been acutely aware of God's favor and presence.

God helped Joseph, too, by sending an angel that same night to confirm what I had already told Joseph. These unexpected developments are still difficult for both of us. However, the joy and anticipation of what is to come far outweigh the awkwardness of our situation.

I have believed and waited for the Messiah all my life. And now, to think, not only will He come in my lifetime, but also I have been chosen to be his earthly mother! I feel so utterly unworthy. It seems at times that this whole thing is a dream. Yet, I know it's real.

And the news of Aunt Elizabeth's pregnancy, too, is just too wonderful. The angel's message about her was almost as amazing as the news of the Messiah. Imagine becoming a mother at her age! She has been called "the barren one" for the last time. It is too much of a coincidence that God has chosen this particular time to bless her and Uncle Zechariah with a child. I am certain these two "miracle" babies are connected somehow.

I have such a need to talk with her. There are so few who I can talk to now. I know Aunt Elizabeth will help me understand. I believe I see her up ahead. Yes, that is my dear aunt standing by the road. Even at this distance, it is obvious she is nearing the end of her waiting time. She looks happy—radiant! I must hurry.

The future is uncertain and it frightens me. But God's promises have been a part of my life as long as I can remember. And God's promises are certain. They are true.

"Dear God, help me to take one day at a time, and leave the future in your hands. Thank you again for your favor."

(Narrative based on Matthew 1:18-24 and Luke 1-2.)

Mary's Answers for Today

Mary did indeed find favor with God. She was chosen above all other women to become the mother of the incarnate Son of God. She is perhaps the best known woman in history. But she was not divine. She admitted her need for a Savior and recognized Jesus as her redeemer when she said, "My spirit doth rejoice in God my Savior." (Luke 1:47) Her example deserves our utmost admiration.

Though we have no idea from scripture about her physical appearance, it is obvious that she possessed an inner beauty and character that allowed her to stand out above all others. Mary is probably the best Biblical example of a woman whose beauty radiated so strongly from within that it made her actual physical features unimportant. This should be the goal of every woman—to possess such a beautiful spirit that her physical attributes, however outstanding or otherwise, diminish into insignificance.

Eminent artists and sculptors throughout history have tried to re-create Mary's appearance. Like them, we can only imagine. We do know, however, that she was poor and lived in Nazareth and was betrothed to Joseph, a carpenter, when the angel Gabriel visited her with the astonishing news that she would conceive the Son of God in her womb.

Have you ever wondered what it would be like to be visited by an angel? That would have been frightening enough. But Gabriel's message to Mary can only be described as shocking. He told her that, though she was still a virgin, she would give birth to the Savior, the Messiah whose coming the Jews had anticipated for so long.

Fortunately, an angel also appeared to Joseph to confirm what Mary had told her betrothed. Joseph, like Mary, had faith in God and was expecting the Messiah. But the story was just too fantastic for him to believe.

In those days, an engagement was as binding as marriage. Their fathers chose a boy and girl for each other when they were very young. Then as the girl neared her mid-teens (the boy was usually a little older), a day of betrothal was set. Both fathers signed a contract, and the groom-to-be gave a gift to his future bride.

The marriage took place within a year, but usually not sooner than nine months. During this time, there was no real courting between the two. They could never be alone together. If the girl became pregnant, the future groom could accuse her before the village council. Obviously, this would have been a very shameful, humiliating, and crushing event for the girl. Or, the man could have a simple divorce drawn up and present it to her at her parents' home. Though she would still be disgraced, at least the scandal would be kept quiet, and she would be under the protection of her parents.[1]

The latter is what Joseph decided to do when he learned Mary was pregnant. It took a heavenly visitation to convince him to go ahead and marry Mary. Scripture does not tell us when the wedding was originally planned to take place, but they obviously had to speed things up with the new developments.

In our time and throughout history, too, hurry-up marriages and weddings for pregnant brides have been far too common. But even today, these kinds of weddings can still be traumatic. Imagine how shocking and disturbing such a wedding would have been in Mary's day. However, it is interesting to note that, although the course of Mary and Joseph's life was drastically altered, God took care of everything. He provided all they needed.

Elizabeth, Mary's aunt, not only confirmed the message, but affirmed and encouraged her. She provided much-needed support during the first months of Mary's pregnancy.

At the time of Jesus' birth, in the midst of a city that was crammed and bustling with people who had come there because of a government decree, God provided a dry, safe stable for Mary and her family. It was humble, but adequate.

Later, wealthy, wise men were miraculously led to the child from distant lands. The gifts they brought to Jesus provided the funds for the family to escape from Herod into Egypt so that Jesus would not be harmed as a result of this king's order that all the baby Jewish boys be killed.

All of these details describe God's characteristic faithfulness. He never calls us to a task without equipping us and providing for us along the way. For Mary, coping with her pregnancy, giving birth to Jesus in a stable and fleeing with her new baby to Egypt to save his life were only the beginning of the challenges she faced as the mother of the Savior.

It took a unique woman to be the mother of God incarnate. God's choice of Mary, a poor, simple peasant girl, is almost as great a mystery as the incarnation itself.

What does it take to be favored by God? Certainly it is a difficult stretch of our imaginations and egos to compare ourselves to this exceptional woman. However, pleasing God and obtaining his approval is possible for all of us. Here are some of the prerequisites to becoming a woman chosen of God.

Profile of the Chosen
Live Close to God and Know His Word

The Lord is with thee.

Luke 1:28

Mary would be the woman who would nurture and train Jesus for the formative years of his life on earth. It was absolutely essential she have the spiritual maturity and closeness with the Father to provide the right environment for the incarnate Christ. She would have to be a great woman of faith who believed God's promises. Every indication is that she possessed such a faith. St. Augustine writes, "Mary first conceived Christ in her heart by faith, before she conceived in the womb." Elizabeth confirms Mary's great faith when she declared, "Blessed is she that believeth."[2]

Mary knew the prophets of old had predicted the coming of a Messiah. She knew He was to be of the line of David. She could recite all the scriptures regarding His birth. I believe she was expecting him in her lifetime. Therefore, though the angel's message of her role in Christ's incarnation surprised and amazed Mary, she was not surprised at the announcement of His coming birth. She not only knew the scriptures, she lived "close to God."

What does it mean to "live close to God?" First, if we are to have a close relationship with God, it must have a beginning. We must, as Mary did, accept Christ as Savior of our lives.

After accepting Christ as Savior, we must continue daily to grow that relationship and live to please God. We must rid ourselves of all the works of the flesh mentioned by Paul in Galatians 5:19-20. Sins such as adultery, witchcraft, anger, murder, jealousy, and strife cannot be a part of our lives, else we will never be counted among the chosen of God.

This is obviously an oversimplification of all it takes to live in close fellowship with God. A friend of mine, Michelle McKinney Hammond, has written a wonderful book, also about Mary, and Michelle gives many more specifics about what God requires of us such as purity, worship, and even rest.[3] The important thing to remember is that we can and must have an intimate relationship with Jesus. And that is doable.

Through His Word, God helps us learn what it takes to live a life that is pleasing to Him. His Word is our guidebook—a set of instructions for living. Throughout scripture we find God's wonderful promises of blessings, we learn what to expect in the future (as Mary learned about the coming Messiah), and we also discover what God expects from us in return. For example, in John 14-16, when Jesus is about to depart for heaven, he leaves his disciples an exciting list of precious legacies such as peace, joy, and the Holy Spirit. However, he also explains his requirement for them to love one another and keep his commands.

In Micah 6:8 we read:

He has showed you, O man, what is good.And what does the Lord require of you?To act justly and to love mercyAnd to walk humbly with your God.

This is pretty basic stuff, but God lets us know in no uncertain terms what he expects our lives to look like. (For more in-depth study on pleasing God, see Chapter 6, "Live by His Rules," in my book, *Growing Your Dreams*,

Bridge-Logos, 2000). The ten commandments
are a good place to begin, but God's word is a
treasure of precious insight into what it takes
to live close to Him and remain in a way of life
that will allow us to be one of His chosen
women.

Live with a Spirit of Expectancy

But take heed to yourselves, lest your hearts
be weighed down with carousing,
drunkenness, and cares of this life,
and that Day come on you unexpectedly.
                           Luke 21:34 (NKJV)

*T*his scripture refers, of course, to the Second
Coming of Christ. But it also describes how
our lives can get so bogged down with the
normal, everyday activities that we become
complacent. We no longer look for Christ's
coming, nor expect His supernatural
intervention in our lives in anyway.

Mary lived with a spirit of expectancy. This
is that added dimension of faith that can make
the difference between "believing" and
"experiencing." Had Mary not lived her life
expecting the Messiah to come, she would not

have been prepared to receive Gabriel's message. She not only believed, she expected it to happen at any moment.

As more and more of God's plan for Jesus was revealed, Mary continued to live with this sense of anticipation. She waited not only with hope, but almost with baited breath for the miracles to begin. She watched, often it seems in silence, and she waited. And, sure enough, when the time was right, she helped thrust Jesus into his ministry.

Mary encouraged her son to intervene at the wedding in Cana at a time when it seems that He did not even realize that the time had come to begin his earthly ministry. But Mary knew (John 2:3-5). She knew because she expected it to happen.

Often, nothing remarkable happens in our lives because we are not expecting anything. If we have a relationship with the Lord and know His Word, we should live each moment with a spirit of expectancy.

Our dreams and calling to do something really significant in God's kingdom can grow dim from the waiting. We become impatient. We have short attention spans. It is so easy to lose our sense of expectancy. We must keep it alive through our steadfast relationship with the Lord and with an intimate familiarity with God's Word. If we are content with a mediocre journey, not expecting the extraordinary or supernatural, chances are, that is exactly what we will get. What should we be expecting? Anything!

First, like Mary, we should expect the fulfillment of the prophecies in God's Word. Second, we should expect God's calling on our lives and for him to choose us for a special mission or task. Third, we should expect the supernatural.

We live in a natural world, and we become so involved in it, we don't expect the supernatural. It is good to remember Christ's miraculous birth and the amazing, supernatural intervention by the angel into Mary's rather dull life. God is still performing miracles today, and, like Mary, we can be chosen to be a part of them. If God calls us, we are more likely to hear his call and respond if we are already living expectantly.

Humbly Accept God's Calling and Plan for Your Life

Mary said,

*I am the Lord's servant, and I am willing
to do whatever he wants.
May everything you said come true.*
Luke 1:38 (TLB)

Mary accepted and believed what the angel said. She never questioned. What amazing faith she must have had! She accepted the prophecies she had heard all her life about the coming Messiah, but she also believed the angel's message that put her right in the middle of those prophecies.

The quality of submission (that word has been so bludgeoned in our day) is perhaps the most difficult virtue for our independent selves to attain. In no other place in the Bible can you find a more perfect example of true submission than in Mary's willingness to go along with God's plan, a plan that, if considered only through our natural eyes, would appear to put Mary in great danger.

It is one thing to say we believe the Bible, but another matter altogether when we are

asked to act out our faith in God's Word—
especially if it puts us out of our comfort zone.
Mary accepted God's Word. She asked only
one logical question about how the pregnancy
could happen. But when the angel answered
her, "All things are possible with God," (Luke
1:37), Mary showed no skepticism or doubt.

Had Mary doubted in her heart, as Sarah of
the Old Testament doubted God's promise,
would God have rejected her and chosen
another?

If you are asked, "Do you believe in God's
protection?" you might quickly respond with,
"Yes." But if you are then asked to put your
life in danger for His purposes, your
affirmation might take a bit longer.

One of the most amazing things about
Mary's story is that she did not worry and fret.
She accepted her calling and left the future in
God's hands. Most of us mothers tend to
worry. I wonder if that is because we do not
know God's word. To worry is not to trust. We
can't have both. Worry takes its toll on our
faces and on our health. We miss one of the
greatest blessings of God—peace and
contentment—when we lack trust.

How much of God's blessing do we miss by doubting Him? If trusting God is hard for you, start small; learn to trust God for small things. As we are willing to act on our seedling faith, God will give us ever-increasing tests to allow that faith to grow. You can be sure Mary had trusted God all her life and had an intimate relationship with Him. She had lived a life of faith. That is why God could trust her with such a huge responsibility.

Mary not only accepted God's calling for her life, she did so humbly. She was certainly humbled by Gabriel's visit. Seeing an angel face-to-face would humble anyone. But Mary maintained her humility throughout.

Jesus' ministry on earth was primarily to the common people. And God in His great wisdom chose a poor girl and a lowly carpenter to raise Jesus in a remote, unremarkable village. Can anything good come out of Nazareth? (John 1:46)

Yes, Mary had humble beginnings, but how easy it would have been for her to become proud. As she saw Jesus growing strong, healthy, wise, and popular, she could have given in to the temptation to brag. What mother wouldn't have been tempted? After all, she had much to brag about.

When God does favor us with a privileged calling or place of prominence, we are so tempted to become proud. Status, position, and leadership are all opportunities to be vessels in God's hands and can allow true greatness to emerge from our ordinary lives. But how often we ruin it by taking the credit and becoming proud. Mary set a beautiful example of true humility in spite of her unique calling and opportunity.

Keep it to Yourself

All who heard the shepherds' story
expressed astonishment,
but Mary quietly treasured these things
in her heart and often thought about them.

Luke 2:18 TLB

Mary kept all the things she knew about Jesus' destiny hidden in her heart. How tempted she must have been at times to reveal what she knew. I'm afraid I might have caved in and blabbed the whole story. I could have ruined Jesus' reputation before he ever began his ministry.

I can see it now. Mary and Jesus are gathered with other mothers and children in the yard. The children are at play and the mothers are talking about their favorite subject, their children. There is always one mother in every group who goes way overboard in bragging about her child. Today she is going at it ad nauseum.

Little "Peter" is the smartest boy in his class. He is the most handsome. He is the best behaved, and he just got the solo in the children's choir. Blah, blah, blah.

Don't you imagine Mary was tempted to say something like, "So what? Jesus will be the Savior of the world. His birth was heralded by heavenly hosts, and a miraculous star led kings to come and worship him."

How do you suppose the other mothers would have responded? Not in a positive way, that's for sure. But Mary did no such foolish thing. She kept quiet.

At twelve years of age, when Jesus was missing and Mary and Joseph found him teaching well-educated men in the temple, I imagine she just filed it away for future reference, too. She had more knowledge and insight into her amazing son than anyone on earth, yet she had the wisdom and self-control to keep it to herself.

Pride and impatience are enemies of God's plan and purpose for our lives. So often when God entrusts us with a special calling, pride raises its ugly head, and our actions prove unworthy of God's confidence. We want to brag to everyone about the new and important job we have been given. Or we foolishly pour out our God-given vision to others, who may not be as happy about it as we are. Often others cannot understand or applaud our calling. That is why it is so important to keep it to ourselves until the timing is right.

I remember when my husband Jerry and I were so strongly called to come to Chicago to put a Christian television station on the air. Jerry was working for Pat Robertson at the time. When Jerry shared our decision and calling with Pat, he was very negative about our leaving CBN and coming to Chicago. He told Jerry it would be impossible to have a successful TV ministry in a city like Chicago. He said it was foolish to try. More than 25 years later, it is obvious he was wrong.

Pat Robertson was and still is one of the greatest men of faith I know. He had stepped out in faith time and again to begin and grow the Christian Broadcasting Network. But that was his vision and calling. He just could not understand Jerry's vision.

Another reason to keep our mouth shut is because when we share our calling with others, we often let ego distort the message. We become so enamored with our calling, our focus changes from obediently following God's direction to rushing forward with the pressure to perform. We then have to live up to our own advertising!

If we could only learn to keep our secret. We must quietly keep God's message in our hearts and give ourselves time to understand and grow into the challenge.

As privileged as Mary's position was, she did not reveal her private knowledge before the proper time. She was patient. We must also learn to wait for God's timing.

Rewards of God's Favor

*W*hen Mary and Joseph returned to Nazareth, they provided a loving though humble home for Jesus. It is important to remember that Mary not only gave birth to Jesus, but she mothered Him for thirty years. She knew He was Divine, yet she did for Him all the earthly, human things a mother does for her son. I believe the greatest privilege and reward of Mary's favor was the unique relationship she had with Jesus. But how strange it must have been for Mary to be the mother of her Lord.

Yes, Mary had a special bond with Jesus that only a mother can have or understand.

She even helped launch His ministry at the wedding at Cana, where she called on Jesus to perform His first miracle. She knew His time had come. A mother knows her child better than anyone—even at 30 years of age.

But the challenges Mary faced during Jesus' upbringing and during His ministry on earth paled in comparison to the utter despair she must have felt at seeing her son beaten, tortured, and killed by an angry mob. The same crowds that had welcomed Him with open arms and palm branches a week before, turned on Him and demanded his death. What a roller coaster of emotions for His poor mother!

Mary's ultimate reward came on that first Easter morning. When Mary glimpsed the gaping, empty tomb and realized her precious son's mission was complete, her joy and gratitude must have been sweet! The words of the angel Gabriel, which she had accepted with such faith and trust, had finally been fulfilled.

What does God's favor look like in our lives? His promises and blessings to those who serve Him are so numerous; no book could possibly list them all.

First and most importantly is the reward of simply being with the Lord. Though Mary's special relationship with Jesus was reserved for her alone, we too can have a close, intimate fellowship with the Lord. And this is the greatest of the blessings God bestows.

As with Mary, God's favor means that He chooses us for His unique plan and purposes; we are blessed with the privilege of being a tool in His loving hands. And this is the reward of a life of significance. A fruitful life and a sense of purpose and mission, as well as a meaning to our lives that is obvious to others as well as to ourselves are some of the signs of God's favor in our lives.

The most beautiful thing about God's favor is that it is not reserved for those who are perfect. Many heroes and heroines of faith had failings and were sinful like all of us. Yet, they were highly favored of God and chosen to fulfill a very special purpose.

King David fell into terrible sin, yet he was called "a man after God's own heart." Rahab was a pagan, an unbeliever, and a harlot, yet she was listed in Hebrews 11 among those remembered for their great faith. And

Abraham's wife, Sarah, failed God time and again. She laughed at God's promise. She became impatient with God's timing and gave her servant girl Hagar to Abraham to bear him a son. Yet God, nonetheless, chose Sara to be the mother of a great nation. In spite of her unbelief, he still used her to fulfill his great plan.

If not the spirituality of Mary, the mother of Jesus, what then does God's favor require? We covered some of the ways to live a life close to God, and these qualities and disciplines are important. However, we must realize it is really nothing that we do that makes us acceptable and useable. It is what He has done. Many of us accept the message of salvation by faith, yet we strive to please God through our good deeds and actions. We feel we must work very hard to be good enough to gain His favor and acceptance.

This idea is more than a misconception. It is a direct insult, a slap in the face of our Savior, who made the ultimate sacrifice on the cross for us and freely offers His unconditional love. The Bible clearly states that it is primarily our faith that pleases God, not our works. (Ephesians 2: 8-9).

Though Mary's role and calling in God's plan was unique, all of us can be just as willing and prepared to do His bidding. We, too, can be worthy instruments in God's creative hands. God's favor is poured out upon anyone who has the faith to believe what he says. It is for all who accept His will unquestionably and travel with quiet submission the unknown paths of obedience. Any woman can have that kind of favor. Any woman can, like Mary, play a part in a miracle.

End Notes

1 Arthur W. Klinck, and Erich H. Kiehl; *Everyday Life in Bible Times*; Concordia Publishing House; St. Louis, MO; pp. 157, 158.

2 Herbert Lockyer, *All the Women of the Bible*, Zondervan Publishing House, p. 94

3 Michelle McKinney Hammond, *Blessed and Highly Favored*, Waterbrook Press, 2001.

Study Guide

More to Explore

*T*he story of young Mary being divinely chosen to be the mother of Jesus is a beautiful picture of God's grace!

To explore more about God's grace and how we, too, are chosen for his purposes, study the following verses and answer the accompanying questions.

- Colossians 3:12
- 1 Peter 2:9
- Romans 3:22-24
- Psalms 33:12
- Acts 22:14

Consider This . . .

What is God's grace?

Can we earn God's grace and favor? Explain.

Knowing you are dearly loved and chosen by God for his special purposes, what should your response be?

Are you familiar enough with God's word to recognize its fulfillment in your own life?

Do you live with a spirit of expectancy?

What are you expecting to happen?

Do you sincerely desire the fulfillment of God's will in your life?

Ask God to make his will clear to you and empower you to accomplish it.

Wise Reflections

Mary is a wonderful role model. She was chosen through God's grace and favor and because of her great trust and love for God.

Upon hearing the angel's message, Mary expressed her overwhelming gratitude in a beautiful, poetic response, "Mary's song" or the "Magnificat."

Read Mary's song in Luke 1:46-55, then write your own song of thanks to God for His loving grace and favor. Be sure to include how God has favored you, what you feel God has chosen you for, and what blessings he has given you through his grace.

Ruth
Friend

Don't make me leave you.
Your people shall be my people,
and your God shall be my God

Ruth 1:16

Ruth
Friend

My name is Ruth. Even though I have lived in Bethlehem for several months now, I am originally from the country of Moab and, therefore, very much a foreigner in the eyes of the Israelites. I came from Moab with Naomi, my mother-in-law, soon after my husband died. Most people would have advised me to stay in my homeland, especially being a widow. Even Naomi, as she returned to her hometown of Bethany, pleaded with me during the journey to return to my parents' home. But I could not leave her. Nor can I refuse to do what she has asked me to do this night.

Although what she has advised me to do is certainly the boldest, most radical thing I have ever done, my dear mother-in-law has convinced me to go to the threshing floor to meet with Boaz. He is one of her husband's relations and a respected man who has shown me great kindness. He has let me glean right behind his reapers. He has given me extra portions of grain and protected me from brazen young men who might have harassed me (or worse yet). Boaz has even asked me more than once to take my afternoon meal with him. He must like me…a little.

If I'm honest with myself, I must admit I am attracted to him. It's true he is older than my first husband, and quite a few years older than I. But there is a youthful energy about him. He's handsome, too, in a mature sort of way. The thing I like the most, though, is his concern for the people around him. He never passes a worker without a smile and a greeting. I've seen the way others respect and love him. But he hasn't actually done anything to lead me to suspect he has any interest in me other than to show kindness to a poor widow. Does Naomi know something I don't?

This plan of hers is truly bizarre! I have put on my best garment, which is still sadly common. I am applying the perfume just like she told me. I have made myself as attractive as possible, but my hand is shaking, and I'm so apprehensive. Can I really be so brazen as to sneak up on the man as he sleeps and crawl under his covers? These Israelite customs are so strange. It seems so much like begging him to marry me. I know it is permissible for a widow to ask a relative to step in for her dead husband, but such things were never done in Moab.

Am I so desperate for a husband? I had given up hope of ever having a husband—or children. I'm not sure if what I feel is anxiety at what I am about to do or simply the excitement of what may, through God's grace, be a new beginning for me. Do I dare let myself hope for a life together with this man? It sounds impossible even inside my head. I do trust Naomi completely, though, and this is what she has instructed me to do. More importantly, I trust Naomi's God—who has since become my God.

The aroma of the freshly cut barley is more pleasant to me than my perfume. The moonlight is beckoning me onward in spite of my pounding heart. I will join my beloved Boaz at the threshing floor… and I will see what happens. (Narrative based on Ruth 1).

Ruth's Answers for Today

*R*uth was correct in thinking Naomi's plan was a bit radical. It was rather brazen, too, but she went to Boaz anyway. Her obedience demonstrated once again the amazing trust and friendship between the two women.

The Book of Ruth, however short in length, is an important one. Not only does it tell us much about Jewish life in ancient Israel during the time of the judges, but it is symbolic of Jesus Christ's redemption of humanity. (It also gives one of the purist examples of friendship and unconditional love in the Bible.) The four short chapters weave a fascinating tale of how one beautiful woman, a poor widow from a pagan land, was ultimately connected with our Redeemer.

We can assume Ruth was physically attractive; at least she was an attractive baby. It is noted in *Personal Names of the Bible* that Ruth's name can mean "something worth seeing" or "friendship" or "female friend."[1]

This close relationship developed between a most unlikely pair, a mother-in-law and her daughter-in-law.

Naomi originally lived with her family in Bethlehem. She had a husband, Elimelech, and two sons, Mahlon and Kilion. There was a famine in the land of Judah at the time and so Elimelech's family decided to move to Moab where food was more abundant and life was easier.

Moab was a pagan country. Everything was different, the people, the customs, and most importantly, the gods. The Moabites did not worship Jehovah, the One True God of the Hebrews.

The Bible says the family "remained there." The Bible doesn't say how long they were there before Elimelech died, but we know the sons were grown because they had married Moabite women. Their names were Ruth and Orpah (no, not Oprah—Orpah).

About ten years later, tragedy struck again; both of Naomi's sons died. Their names Mahlon and Kilion mean "sickly" and "failing," so perhaps they had never been well, but for whatever reason, they died and left Naomi alone with her two daughters-in-law.

With her husband and sons dead, Naomi decided to return to her homeland of Judah. She had heard that there was plenty of food there. Ruth and Orpah started the journey with her, but along the way, Naomi realized that the younger women would be better off staying in Moab.

She set a wonderful example for these two young women there on the road that day. In spite of her deep grief and heartache, she demonstrated her love and concern for her daughters-in-law. And Ruth reciprocated her gesture of kindness a hundred times over. Let's examine the elements of true friendship portrayed so dramatically by Naomi and Ruth.

Profile of a True Friend
Put the needs of others before your own

...Why don't you return to your parents' home instead of coming with me? And may the Lord reward you for your faithfulness to your husbands and to me. And may he bless you with another happy marriage.
Ruth 1:8,9 TLB

The three women had started on the journey together, but Naomi changed her mind. She realized the girls would have a bleak future if they stayed with her. She not only freed them from any obligation on her part, she gave them her blessing. This was not just a half-hearted gesture. Naomi insisted they return to their parents' homes.

This was a huge decision for Naomi to make. She had to be a fairly old woman by this time. To make another move back to Judah at her age must have been difficult. But with the young women at her side, it would not have been such a lonely journey or such a dark future. But she put the needs of Ruth and Orpah before her own. Even while she was going through emotional and spiritual upheaval in her own life, in the throes of horrible grief, she was still thinking of others.

How often in the midst of our busy lives do we prove to be only "fair weather friends?" We look at friendship as a luxury reserved for our spare time and only if everything is going well. How many of us genuinely care enough about others to put their needs before our own? This concern for others during time of personal difficulty is the mark of true friendship.

Be Willing to Sacrifice

Entreat me not to leave you,
Or to turn back from following after you;
For wherever you go, I will go;
And wherever you lodge, I will lodge;
Your people shall be my people,
And your God, my God.

Where you die, I will die,
there will I be buried.

The Lord do so to me, and more also,
If anything but death parts you and me.

Ruth 1:16-17 NKJV

*T*he girls began to weep when Naomi asked them to stay behind. They wanted to return to Judah with this woman who had become like their own mother. But Naomi insisted, and finally Orpah decided to remain in Moab and return to her family.

Ruth, however, refused to leave her mother-in-law. There on the dusty road leaving Moab, Ruth made one of the most famous speeches in the Bible, one that has been repeated thousands of times. In a beautiful, poetic response, filled with emotion, Ruth steadfastly refused to part with her mother-in-law. What an incredible bond they must have developed over those ten years they had known each other!

Ruth, though a beautiful woman in the physical sense, also had a beauty of spirit, which began to reveal itself at this important time in her life. It is the same inner quality that later attracted Boaz. In Ruth 2:11 he says, "Yes, I know (you are a foreigner)...I also know about all the love and kindness you have shown your mother-in-law since the death of your husband...."

Ruth made the decision to stay with Naomi, even though her future in Judah promised nothing but bleakness. What were the sacrifices she was making for Naomi? What did it mean for her future?

She was leaving her homeland and all that was familiar to her. She was leaving her parents, siblings, and friends and moving to a strange land with many more rules and restrictions than Moab. She would be living among strangers, except for Naomi.

She was committing herself to a life of poverty. She and Naomi had no means of support.

She was resigning herself to remain unmarried. Naomi even pointed this out, saying that her chances of finding a husband would be much better in Moab. By making this choice, Ruth also accepted the fact that she would remain childless. In Israel especially, being without children was considered a curse and a disgrace. However, Ruth was willing to give up any future children she might have had in order to stay with Naomi.

I wonder how many of us would make such sacrifices for a friend? Perhaps you cannot relate to Ruth's radical act of loyalty. It is easier to understand if we bring the scenario to a present day situation. What about the decision to take into your home an aging parent or a sick relative? I know of a woman in Texas who put off her wedding for years because she was caring for her mother in her home and did not feel she could ask her fiancé to make this sacrifice with her. Her mother eventually passed away, but the wedding never took place.

I interviewed a woman who quit her corporate job to stay home and care for her mother who had Alzheimer's. She lovingly attended her mom's every need for 14 years before the disease finally took her mother's life. She affectionately referred to her mother as "her fading angel."[2]

There are opportunities, at some point in our lives, for each of us to make sacrifices for a friend or family member. This is where the line is drawn and the selfless, inner spirit is put to the test. The women I have mentioned, and thousands more like them, are truly beautiful in the ways that matter most.

Love Unconditionally

...my daughters; oh, how I grieve for you
that the Lord has punished me
in a way that injures you.

Ruth 1:13

*T*he verse above is one of several that reveals Naomi's emotional condition when she returned to Bethlehem. The statement was not true, but it revealed her frame of mind at the time. Naomi was having a major pity party, believing that God was punishing her and causing her daughters-in-law to suffer because of her. Despite her personal pain, she had put Ruth and Orpah's needs before her own, but she was certainly dealing with serious issues in her life.

Ruth's willingness to remain faithful to Naomi when she was going through such a rough time proves she was not just a "fair weather friend." She had been extremely close to her for ten years. She had seen her good days and bad days, which we all have. However, this time in Naomi's life had to be the lowest point. Naomi had gone through a terrible crisis and was so depressed she was ready to change her name from "sweet" to "bitter" (Ruth 1:20). Yet Ruth loved her unconditionally.

The test of true friendship is to love in the bad times as well as the good. We tend to seek out friends that are fun, make us feel better, or can give something back to us. We tend to shy away from the "needy" or "troubled" people who will be higher maintenance. We sense the friendship will be one-sided, and we choose to take a pass.

It is easier to understand unconditional love between a parent and child. All of us who have had wayward teenagers or adult children understand what it means to keep on loving— in spite of the hurt, the disappointment and heartache. Most of us would agree, there is almost nothing a child could do to us to destroy our love for them.

I remember hearing Nancy Heche, mother of the actress Ann Heche, describe on our television program how painful it was for her when she heard that Ann was in a relationship with Ellen DeGeneres. Ann hurt her mother time and time again by the things she said, sometimes on national TV. However, Nancy continued to love her and make an effort to be a part of her life. Though she passionately disapproved of Ann's lifestyle, this did not affect her love for her daughter.

It is a bit harder to grasp the concept of the unconditional love of God for his creation. We understand a mother's love, but can we fit our minds and hearts around the idea of a sinless, loving Christ being crucified by the very people He is dying to redeem? Then, to hear Him declare, "Father, forgive them, for they know not what they do!" This extreme love blows our minds and challenges our definitions of love.

Since we are human and imperfect, we can never hope to achieve pure, unconditional love like Christ demonstrated. However, if you allow Christ to love through you, you can become a better friend than ever before. You can be there for others, even at the darkest hour of their lives, even when they are being completely unlovable.

Have you ever wondered why Ruth was willing to make such personal sacrifices for this older woman? Obviously, an unusual friendship had developed between the two women. But I also believe Ruth had embraced

Naomi's God, Jehovah. She even said as much: "Your God, [shall be] my God." Ruth had seen something in Naomi's religion that was more meaningful to her than all the pagan gods of Moab. I believe Ruth's sacrificial love for Naomi was a result of her relationship with the One True God. It is only through relationship with Christ that we can be a friend who loves unconditionally.

Look Beyond the Surface to See the Real Needs

...Almighty God has dealt me bitter blows. I went out full and the Lord has brought me home empty; why should you call me Naomi when the Lord has turned his back on me and sent such calamity!

Ruth 1:20b 21

Naomi was furious with God. She felt He had treated her unjustly, turned His back on her, and sent her tragedy as a way of punishing her. Through her grief and depression, Naomi had totally lost her perspective.

One important benefit of close friendships is that a friend's perspective can put a completely different spin on things. I have often been upset, disappointed, or worried as I shared my concerns with my husband—or perhaps a close friend. A few well-placed words and a hug from them gave me a totally different perspective. Things just didn't seem so bad after all.

An old Christian song says, "He [God] looked beyond my faults and saw my need." God is better at seeing our needs than we humans are. We tend to see only the outward symptoms or behavior patterns, and dislike or totally reject a person based on those actions.

But sometimes we simply do not take the time to get involved in the life of a person who is struggling. It's just so much simpler to pick another friend, a healthier one, or maybe decide to not bother with friendships at all.

I have found that usually there is a definite reason for a person's negative behavior or point of view. They may have been made to feel inadequate in other key relationships, forcing them to search elsewhere for affirmation. Or they could (like Naomi) still be healing from the pain of loss, abuse, or rejection.

I believe Ruth refused to leave her friend because she looked beyond the surface to identify her real needs. What were Naomi's needs as she set off for Bethlehem?

Naomi had a material need. She had no income and no means of support. Perhaps Ruth felt responsible to see that Naomi had enough food.

Naomi had an emotional need. She was depressed and in despair. She had lost her husband and both her children within a few years. She was still deep in the throws of grief where rational thinking is often absent. She was feeling guilty, as the surviving person often does. She blamed herself for some unknown sin that had called down God's wrath on her and her daughters-in-law. She was not in a healthy mental state. How could Ruth leave her while she was still so fragile?

Naomi had a spiritual need. Naomi was going through the anger stage of grieving. She was mad at God. Her faith, which had always been so important to her, was being threatened. Ruth probably felt very grateful to Naomi for introducing her to the one true God. She now wanted to help her friend and spiritual mentor regain her spiritual equilibrium and become again the strong woman of faith she had once been. Ruth knew she only needed a little time.

I challenge you to look beyond the surface of a person's actions and personality and try to discern their real needs. We can only be a true friend if we become involved enough in the lives of others to see beyond the surface.

The Rewards of Friendship

*H*aving a close and genuine friendship (even only one) is a precious gift from God. I just mentioned one benefit is having someone to go to for a different perspective, someone who will listen to your problems and be honest with you. Another reward, of course, is the joy and happiness that person brings into your life, and the fun that can be had with someone you totally trust and enjoy being with. A good friend will be a support when you face tragedy and heartache, perhaps even to the point of self-sacrifice. A true friend will tolerate you when you are being a brat, and take the time to discover what is really bothering you. The rewards of friendship are too numerous to mention here. Let's take a look at how Ruth was rewarded for her faithfulness.

When the two widows made their way back to Bethlehem, Ruth immediately began taking care of her friend. She took the only job available to her—gleaning in the fields. There were probably many fields Ruth could have chosen, but she "just happened" to choose a field belonging to Boaz, a close relative of Naomi's. Little did Ruth realize that decision would impact her "bleak" future in a most dramatic way!

Boaz, the owner of the field, noticed Ruth immediately. She may have been a beautiful woman, but Boaz was also attracted to her because of her inner beauty. It could have been because she was such a hard worker, or because she portrayed a quiet and lovely spirit. Though he was very kind to her, he was slow to reveal his deep affection for Ruth. Perhaps it was because of their age difference, or because she was a foreigner. Naomi was taking it all in, and knew she would have to help move things along a bit.

Naomi came up with a plan that was to change both their lives and futures. Thus we find Ruth at the beginning of this chapter, nervously getting ready to go to Boaz. Why would Naomi ask her to do such a thing? Due to an ancient custom, middle-eastern women would often go to bed at night by climbing under the covers from the bottom of the bed. This was a symbol of respect for the husband, and was a way of asking for his protection and care.

When Boaz awakened around midnight and found Ruth lying at his feet, he knew she was asking him to be her protector and husband. Instead of scolding her for her behavior, he complimented her for her kindness and for not chasing younger men. It was exactly what he needed to move him to action. Boaz proceeded quickly the next morning to take the necessary steps to make Ruth his wife.

Naomi was rewarded for her friendship to Ruth when Ruth presented her with Boaz's son, a precious grandson she never expected to have. Ruth, however, was blessed beyond her wildest dreams. Everything Ruth had given up was restored.

She had given up her financial security, and now she was rich. Resigning herself to remain unmarried and childless, she now had a distinguished husband and a newborn son.

She had left her homeland, but now had a new home. She had renounced her pagan gods to serve the one true God, who blessed her with the unimaginable privilege of being in the genealogy of Jesus. Obed, her son, was the grandfather of King David. Very few Gentiles show up in the lineage of Jesus, and Ruth was one of them.

Ruth demonstrated many beautiful inner qualities such as humility, industriousness, obedience, and courage. However, she is remembered most for her loyalty and commitment as a true friend.

One sure way of becoming more beautiful is to become this kind of faithful friend—to at least one person. In our busy, self-absorbed culture, it takes time, commitment, and real effort to develop and nurture true and lasting friendships. If you make the effort, however, you will, like Ruth, always receive far more than you give.

Study Guide

More to Explore

*R*uth sacrificed her own comfort and security to remain with Naomi. Even though her mother-in-law had become bitter and self-pitying, Ruth realized it was then that Naomi needed her most.

It is a rare friend who is willing to make such sacrifices, willing to put a friend's needs first.

Read the following Scripture verses to expand your study of friendship.

- Proverbs 27:9
- Ecclesiastes 4:9-12
- 1 John 3:16
- Proverbs 18:24

Consider This

List the five top qualities you possess that
make you a good friend to others.

_____

_____

What is the difference between being a true
friend and just a friendly acquaintance?

_____

How is giving of yourself and your time a key
difference between these two?

_____

When was a time you might not have acted as
a true friend to someone?

_____

Upon reflection, what could you have done
differently?

_____

In what ways do vulnerability, risk-taking, and trust work together to strengthen and solidify a friendship?

Think of a friend or acquaintance who is not very pleasant to be around. Have you taken the time to look beyond the surface to discern her real needs? Ask God to give you a genuine love and concern for her.

Wise Reflections

Remember the old campfire song, " Make new friends, but keep the old; one is silver and the other's gold." It was a fun song to sing, but when it comes to true friendship, no amount of silver or gold can compare with its value. Friendships in the Bible saved nations and created kingdoms, forged alliances, and joined forces in battle.

Through the friendship between Ruth and Naomi, God's will for the nation of Israel was accomplished as he placed this foreign woman in direct line to David and through David to Jesus, our best and truest friend.

Ruth's amazing devotion and loyalty to Naomi were greatly rewarded when she married Boaz. Though Boaz made Ruth a wealthy woman, her true wealth lay in her friendship with Naomi and her love of the Lord.

Think of the many qualities it takes to be a true friend; then list those qualities according to their beginning letters. For example, the "F" in the word "friendship" might stand for faithfulness.

F   faithfulness

R   _____

I   _____

E   _____

N   _____

D   _____

S   _____

H   _____

I   _____

P   _____

Now write a brief thank you note to God for the true friends in your life. Be sure to thank God specifically for those traits that set them apart from "friendly acquaintances."

Hannah
Mother

O Lord of Heaven,
if you will answer my prayer
and give me a son,
then I will give him back to you.

1 Samuel 1:11

Hannah
Mother

My name is Hannah. My son, the little angel cradled in my arms, is Samuel. The hour is late, but I cannot bear to carry him to his bed and retire myself. This evening must last as long as possible.

As he peacefully sleeps against me, he has never looked more vulnerable—or more charming. My breath catches in my throat as I admire his dark curls framing his face and his long lashes that fan his cheeks. He is a beautiful child, and he is still so young!

Our home is in the mountains of Ephraim, but we are staying in rented quarters in Shiloh. We have made our yearly journey to the temple to bring our offerings and our prayers of repentance to the Lord of Hosts. This is my first journey to Shiloh in three years. It was at the temple, just a short distance from here, where it all began. It seems like only yesterday. How have the years flown by so quickly?

Eli, the priest, saw me in the temple and thought I was drunk! I suppose the unhappiness on my face and the intensity of my prayers appeared strange. Even my own husband, who loves me, could not understand my sadness then.

I so desperately wanted a child that I bargained with God, and I would do it again. I didn't make the vow lightly, and I have never regretted it. I knew it would not be easy to surrender my only child to God's service, but I wouldn't take back one single word of my vow to the Lord. I still remember my prayer that day:

> *O Lord of heaven, if you will look down upon my sorrow and answer my prayer and give me a son, then I will give him back to you, and he'll be yours for his entire lifetime, and his hair shall never be cut.*
>
> I Samuel 1:11

When Eli finally realized I was not drunk in the temple that day, but only praying desperately for a child, my embarrassment and distress turned to joy as he pronounced his blessing upon me. And faith was instantly birthed in my heart; I knew this was my time. No more tears, no more fasting.

I hadn't realized though how small and defenseless my boy would be when the time came for me to part with him. How could I have known then how much a mother can love her child or how this son would become to me dearer than my own life?

Still, I know in my heart God has a higher purpose for my little Samuel. And I must trust God to take care of him now. This temple will become his home instead of our cozy house in Ramah. Samuel's little bed at our house will be empty; he will sleep among the stately vessels of the Holy Place and under the same roof as the ark of God. What a privilege my Samuel will have to learn of God's truths firsthand and participate in the holy traditions of the Lord's priests. There can be no greater joy for me than to know my only son is in the service of God— even at his tender age.

No, I cannot be selfish. I must keep my vow to God and leave this place with empty arms. It will be all right. My calm resolve and sense of peace surprise me. Samuel's destiny lies here in Shiloh. I know God will give me the strength I need for the lonely days ahead.

Sleep. Sleep on my precious child. The dawn will be here soon, and then we must say, "Goodbye."

But for now, have pleasant dreams…and let your mother steal one last kiss.

(Narrative based on I Samuel 1, 2)

Hannah's Answers for Today

*C*an you imagine the agonizing conflict in **Hannah's heart** on that night, the last one she would have to cradle her young son in her arms? What a bittersweet moment it must have been. Samuel had been the apple of her eye since his birth. She doted on him, savoring each tender moment as he passed through infancy and became a mischievous toddler. Every milestone in his development, each tiny discovery with him was like a special gift—an unexpected joy for a woman who had been barren.

Hannah must have mothered Samuel with the special care and gratitude of a mother who has waited a long time for a child. And their separation while he was still a young child must have been difficult for her. But Hannah must have been filled with pride and eager anticipation for the yet-unknown purpose and plan God had in store for her first-born son.

The time had come at last. for Hannah. After staying home with Samuel for three years while the rest of her family made their annual trip to Shiloh to worship the Lord,

Hannah now returned to Shiloh to worship with her family for the first time since giving birth to Samuel. Samuel was now weaned, so Hannah brought him to the temple just as she promised God she would.

Children were seldom weaned until they were two or three years of age in those days. Hannah's reluctance to wean this child would have made the LeLeche League proud, I'm sure. But when she could no longer delay the inevitable, she fulfilled her vow to God.

You may not think very highly of Hannah's bargaining with God to get her prayer answered. The whole idea of making promises to God in order to receive something is rather distasteful to evangelical Christians today. However, if we are honest, all of us have yielded to the temptation to pray something like: God, if you will only let me pass this test, I promise to study very hard the rest of the semester and be more faithful to church; God, if you'll heal this sick child, I'll be a better mother; I'll never lose my temper, etc. etc.

Before we judge Hannah too harshly, it is good to understand how vows were looked upon in Hannah's day. Making vows to God is an ancient custom documented as far back in the Bible as Job. The Jews and heathen nations alike regularly practiced it. There was no Jewish law requiring vows to God, but if you made one of your own free will, the law required you to fulfill it. Deuteronomy 23:21 and 22 states this clearly, and in no way indicates that God disapproved of this religious act.

The vows usually involved a gift or promise of a gift given to God in return for his goodness or blessing. As in Hannah's case, the vow could also be made in anticipation of receiving the blessing or answer to prayer. The gift or offerings dedicated to God could be houses or lands, animals for sacrifices, or the person making the vow himself, his slaves or his children.

One of the most common types of vows was the Nazarite vow. This is what Hannah was promising to God if He would give her a son. We find several Biblical examples of Nazarites besides Samuel, including Samson, John the Baptist, and, as some scholars believe, perhaps Saul, as well. The Nazarite would be consecrated to God, and his devotion would be symbolized by never having his hair cut. He was also never allowed to touch a dead body. The regulations regarding this type of vow are detailed carefully in Numbers 6. This practice was not a novelty during Hannah's time; it was common practice.[1]

So Hannah's decision to dedicate her future son as a Nazarite was commendable, especially in light of the sacrifice she was willing to make by bringing him to serve in the temple at such a young age. Hannah chose the most extreme, radical service to God she could think of. It was the single most religious or spiritual act possible in her circumstances. Her commitment is to be admired, and God rewarded that commitment by answering her prayer, giving her a son.

The natural tendency for most mothers is to put their children first—before anything. This is understandable since newborns come into the world totally helpless and dependent on us mothers for their very survival. We easily get into the habit of complete devotion to our offspring at the expense of all other areas of our lives. This is not necessarily a bad thing as long as it's necessary and kept in balance.

However, the Bible is pretty clear on how we should set our priorities. We are told to love the Lord our God with all our hearts, souls, and minds, and love our neighbors as ourselves. It is obvious who our first priority should be—God. I believe that the "neighbor" category covers our husbands, our children, and others around us. The "as ourselves" phrase indicates we should have healthy self-love and allow for attention to our own needs, as well.

Godly parents need to intentionally put their love of the Lord ahead of even their devotion to their own children. We may never have to give up our three-year-old and leave him in the care of strangers as Hannah did. However, every mother's devotion to God is tested through her children time and again throughout her life.

Hannah's story exemplifies not only her primary devotion to the Lord, but also the Biblical principal of receiving through giving. It is seemingly a paradox, but when we surrender anything to God, we ultimately receive more than we have given up. This idea is clearly stated by Jesus in Luke 17: 33:

> *Whoever seeks to save his life will lose it,*
> *and whoever loses his life will preserve it.*

There are many scriptural demonstrations of this principal, but one that is particularly meaningful in terms of God's role in the mother-son relationship is the story of Moses and his mother Jocabed. In order to save the life of her son, Jocabed surrendered him to the Nile River, which symbolized death since the Pharaoh of her day had ordered that all the Jewish baby boys were to be drowned.

When she could no longer hide her beloved son, Jocabed placed his little basket in those crocodile-infested waters as a total act of faith in God. She gave him up and trusted God completely with his future.

In a similar way, present day mothers relinquish their children to a sin-infested world, a liberal, secular university or even a life of service on a foreign mission field. Our test could be allowing our wayward children the freedom to rebel, to leave the faith they have grown up in, and yet still continue to love and accept these children unconditionally.

These challenges to a mother's trust in God can be compared, at least in some small way, to the faith of Hannah as she left her little boy at the temple that day.

We must dedicate our children to God, pray for them, and leave their futures in God's hands. This is why I love the ritual of dedicating children to the Lord in a formal ceremony at church. It is scriptural, and it is a symbol of the parents offering their children to God, whatever that may later require of them. It is not a guarantee of the child's salvation— but an act of dedication on the part of the parents. It's a vow that we parents must take seriously.

Are we mothers who are truly willing to give up our children to God's plans for their lives?

The loving God we serve does not require the death of our children on an altar of fire, a practice that was common among pagans in ancient cultures. Infant sacrifice, a practice so abhorrent that we today cannot even imagine any mother participating in it, was commonly practiced; it is documented in the Bible, as well as by historians and archaeologists.

Historian Thomas Cahill, in his book on the history of Christianity in Ireland, mentions a discovery by archaeologists Anne Ross and Don Robins of the remains of a sacrificed Druid priest. They believe he had come from Ireland around the time the Romans were asserting their control, and he offered himself as a sacrifice to the gods for the defeat of the Romans. His body was found among the bodies of several men dug out of the bogs of England in an amazing state of preservation due to the chemical properties of the peat in the bog. According to these archaeologists, the men's faces were at peace, almost smiling. Their hands were uncalloused, the nails beautifully manicured.

It is not so hard to understand why pagan cultures would stoop so such extremes if you understand their theology and view of god. They viewed him as an arbitrary trickster, a bad parent who could be coaxed, flattered and manipulated. He was a cruel and arbitrary master, demanding someone's blood. If belief in such a god is strong and primitive enough, it is not difficult to see how it could lead to human sacrifice. Here, take him, not me.[2]

For pagans who lived in a society where human sacrifice was practiced, including the sacrifice of their own infants, can you imagine what a joyful message it must have been to learn the Good News of Christ, who had made the final and supreme sacrifice? Blood sacrifices were no longer required—not even animal sacrifices. How gratefully they must they have received the message Paul expresses in his letter to the Philippians:

> *Though he possessed divine estate He was not jealous to retain equality with God. He cast off his inheritance, and took the nature of a slave and walked as man among men. He emptied himself to the last and was obedient to death—even the death of the cross.*
>
> Philippians 2:6-8

This Good News of a God who sacrificed His Son for us was the welcome message St. Patrick presented to the Irish. It was a message that freed them to abandon their gory altars of human sacrifice and become, themselves, living sacrifices to a loving God. They could say, "He does not hate us, he loves us." No wonder the Irish eagerly embraced Christianity.[3]

Let us never forget the loving, patient, understanding nature of the God we serve as it relates to our children. He loves them even more than we do and has a higher purpose for their lives than we can even imagine. When we dedicate our children to the Lord, we may never know the far-reaching effects of our vow.

Samuel's life, which was devoted to the Lord from the time he was weaned, is a great example of a living sacrifice. But did Hannah know what her choices as a mother would mean to the Jewish nation?

Her beautiful, prophetic prayer, which she delivered as she left her beloved son at the temple, predicted radical change for Israel:

> *My heart rejoices in the Lord,…The bows of the mighty men are broken, and those who stumbled are girded with strength… The Lord makes poor and makes rich; He brings low and lifts up.*
>
> 1 Samuel 2:1-10 NKJV

In her song of praise to the Lord, Hannah does not refer to her personal circumstances of once being barren, or giving birth, or sacrificing her son. She has moved beyond her own personal situation to that of the community. She speaks of the future, not her barren past. She may not be aware of all she is saying, but in her heart she knows her son is the key. What a joyful moment this must have been for her in spite of her sadness over her eminent separation from her son.

Hannah's song is very similar to the song of praise that Mary uttered when she was told she would become the mother of the Savior. Note the parallels between the two women's praises:

> *My soul magnifies the Lord,*
> *and my spirit has rejoiced*
> *in God my Savior…*
>
> *He has put down the mighty from their*
> *thrones, and exalted the lowly.*
>
> *He has filled the hungry with good things,*
> *and the rich he has sent away empty.*
>
> Luke 1:46-55

Jesus' mother Mary like Samuel's mother Hannah speaks of the future. Hannah's song heralds the future of Israel; it predicts the anointing of David as king, and the defeat of the Philistines, just as Jesus' birth heralded the salvation of mankind.

Hannah's song, like Mary's, dealt with far more than her personal situation. These women's prophetic proclamations extended to their community, their nation and ultimately to all of mankind.

And there are many parallels in the lives of Samuel and Jesus. Samuel and his service to Israel is an example of the Christ who will come to the world through Israel. Samuel represents in the Old Testament the redemption of the Jewish nation, just as Jesus became the Savior of the world. The Bible even says of Samuel,

> *And the child Samuel grew in stature,*
> *and in favor both with the Lord and men.*
> 1 Sam. 2:26

These are almost the exact words spoken of Jesus.

But how could Hannah have known what her sacrificial act of dedication would mean for the future?

The story of Hannah and Samuel occurs at a transitional period in Israel's history. The leadership was changing from judges to kings. Samuel became the last judge of Israel and issued in the period of the kings. Samuel's role in this pivotal moment in history is huge. During his lifetime, he was instrumental in several critical events in the history of Israel. He was a godly priest who followed after a long line of corrupt priests. He became the recognized leader of the nation until he anointed Saul King. Although Samuel had resisted the idea of a king for Israel and was hurt that the people were not satisfied with his leadership, he followed God's instructions to give them what they wanted and to make Saul king.

Samuel helped turn God's people from idolatry to worship of the true God once again, and the Ark of the Covenant was eventually returned to its proper place. The Philistines, who had tormented God's people for years, experienced the beginning of the end as a result of Samuel's help. They were finally defeated once and for all during David's reign. And the ultimate act of Samuel's life came when he anointed David, God's chosen, as King of Israel.

But when Samuel was still a boy growing up in the temple, it must have been sad for brave Hannah to travel to Shiloh once a year to worship her Lord and visit her son, bringing a little coat she had lovingly made for him. Perhaps you think you could never be that strong or dedicated to God. Hopefully, most of us will never have to be. But we all face individual challenges of obedience regarding our children.

If we are willing to offer our little ones to the Lord, He will equip us and give us the wisdom to succeed. Let's look at some of the attitudes and practical steps necessary to be that kind of mother.

Profile of a Wise Mother

Approach God Boldly with Your Needs

One evening after supper,
when they were at Shiloh,
Hannah went over to the Tabernacle…
She was in deep anguish and was crying
bitterly as she prayed to the Lord.

1 Samuel 1: 9,10

No matter what your age or experience in parenting, no matter how many how-to books you've read or how many degrees you hold, you just cannot expect to be an effective mother without God's help. This is a fact of life. The world we live in holds many dangers and pitfalls for our children. We need the intervention of a supernatural God.

Our relationship with the Lord must be so intimate that we can go to him daily, many times a day if necessary, on behalf of our children. I'm not speaking of the shallow, faithless dialogues we spoke of earlier: God, if you'll help me pass this test, I'll study harder." No, I mean our prayers must be the result of a genuine faith in and understanding of God's power to bring change and answers to our needs. Our prayers must be sincere petitions to a personal God who passionately loves our children and has promised never to leave us or forsake us.

It is not enough to communicate with God only when our children are in trouble. The prayers that bring results are those that flow naturally out of regular communication with the Savior, who is also our best friend, our comforter, and our source. When we maintain that kind of close spiritual union with the Lord, we can come boldly and unashamedly to Him with our needs, no matter how great or small they may be.

I am fully convinced through God's word and also from many personal experiences as a mother of more than 30 years that God is meticulously interested in even the smallest detail of our lives—especially concerning our children.

Hannah was not embarrassed or ashamed to ask for a child though some said she was being ungrateful with the blessings God had already bestowed on her, such as a loving husband. But Hannah knew what she wanted, and she asked for it. We, too, should not hesitate to ask God for our needs and desires.

As a mother of two great, healthy little boys, I still had an ache in my heart for a daughter. My husband and I made the decision to proceed with adopting a baby girl, and I prayed for God to bring the right child into our home. The result was my wonderful daughter Vanessa, who remains, as ever, one of the greatest joys of my life, my best friend, and the mother of my four precious grandchildren.

Before we adopted Vanessa, people told me to leave well enough alone, to be grateful for my two healthy children. But I had a deep desire for a daughter, and I was not ashamed to ask God for what I wanted.

The words of Psalms 37:4 and 5 are a great encouragement to take our desires, needs, and problems to the Lord and expect an answer.

Delight yourself also in the Lord, and he shall give you the desires of your heart. Commit your way to the Lord, Trust also in Him, and he shall bring it to pass.

Of course, we need to understand that God knows what is best for us and our children and can also answer by saying, "No." However, just as we want our children to feel free to ask us for what they want, even though sometimes we must say, "No," God also wants us to ask Him. There is no need too small, too insignificant, or too narrow to take to the Lord in prayer.

Whether you are concerned about a seriously ill child, money for summer camp, the decision of where to send your kids to school, or what sports you should allow them to participate in, you can take these needs to the Lord. Do so boldly and with faith.

Expect To Be Misunderstood

Eli noticed her mouth moving
as she was praying silently
and, hearing no sound,
thought she had been drinking.
"Must you come here drunk?"
he demanded.
"Throw away your bottle."

1 Samuel 1: 12-14

*P*oor Hannah! It was not bad enough that she was heartbroken over having no children and tormented by her husband's other wife; now she was thought to be drunk in the house of the Lord! She was horribly misunderstood.

The fact is, as mothers we might as well get used to the idea that we will be misunderstood. Often, our husbands, friends, parents, and our own children will disagree and struggle with the decisions we make. I wonder how little Samuel felt that morning when he had to say goodbye to his mother. How could he possibly understand Hannah's decision? The Bible does not speak of Samuel's feelings at that moment, but my heart breaks to think of that fragile little guy standing in the door waving to his mother, with no one to comfort him except the elderly priest Eli.

Though there is wisdom in much counsel, and the husband certainly partners with the wife in raising children, there are times when only a mother knows what is best for her child. We mothers simply have insight and a perception for our offspring that no one else can understand, and therein lies the potential for misunderstanding. Whether it is a decision to choose a private school, or home school, or say, "no," to an extra-curricular activity, a mother can just expect to be misunderstood. But that should not influence the decision she knows is right for her child.

A dear friend of mine, Linda, gave birth to her third child who, because of an erroneous medical procedure, lost his hearing. As mother of this profoundly deaf child, she and her husband Mike had to make a decision about his education and training. There was much pressure to teach Ronnie signing, but Linda and Mike wanted Ronnie to be a part of the hearing world. He constantly tried to speak.

They knew if he learned sign language, he would probably never speak. So they found him a retired teacher who taught Ronnie the oral method of communication. Ronnie never learned signing and was never really a part of the deaf community. Linda was sorely misunderstood and received a lot of criticism for her decision.

But Ronnie became a great lip reader, learned to speak surprisingly well, and Linda actually accompanied him to school for most of his education, mouthing the words of the teachers to Ronnie. (Talk about a sacrificing mother! But that is another story.) He not only kept up his grades, but also excelled in football, and went on to graduate from a local junior college. Today he is happily married (to a hearing person), and he runs a very successful business.

A few years ago, with the introduction of the cochlear implant technology, Ronnie learned he was a perfect candidate for the surgery. He is now beginning to hear sounds for the first time in his life, and he is expected to develop about 80 percent hearing over time. It is truly a medical miracle. However, if

Ronnie had not been taught the oral method of communication and learned to speak when he was young, he would not have been a candidate for this procedure. He would never hear his wife say, "I love you," or hear the cry of his first baby.

Linda was misunderstood, but she persevered because she knew in her heart what was best for her son. And she was right.

Learn To Be Tough-Skinned and Love Unconditionally

Peninnah, Elkanah's other wife,
made matters worse for Hannah
by taunting her about being barren.
Every year it was the same—
Peninnah scoffing and laughing at Hannah
as they went to Shiloh,
making her cry so much she couldn't eat.

1 Samuel 1:6, 7

*O*ne of the saddest parts of Hannah's story is the abuse she was forced to endure from Peninniah—the other woman.

Polygamy, though an acceptable practice in the Hannah's time, has never been anything but trouble. Perhaps Hannah, on finding she could not produce children for Elkanah, encouraged her husband to take another wife as Sarah did Abraham.

In any case, Hannah had the mixed blessing of being the wife Elkanah loved most. But his preference for Hannah probably fired Peninniah's jealousy and made her more hateful toward's Hannah. And her cruelty towards Hannah came to a head each year when the family journeyed to Shiloh to worship. What Hannah experienced would have been, for a woman today, like having a bitter relative ruin every family get together at a special occasion like Christmas.

Hannah was so distressed she couldn't eat and she wept bitterly. It doesn't appear that Hannah cried for attention or sulked. She was profoundly heartbroken and disappointed, but she did exactly the right thing. She took her feelings and needs to God. Hannah wasn't tough-skinned enough to deal with Peninniah.

In addition to being misunderstood, mother's have to expect a certain amount of abuse. It can be from a mother-in-law, an insensitive husband, or others, but the unkindness is often from those they love the most—their children.

For the sake of a happy home and for the sake of our children, we must become tough-skinned. We must learn to love unconditionally. Throughout our lives we will be hurt by our children. Most of the time it is unintentional. However, anyone with grown children knows painfully well how cruel rebellious teenagers can be to their mothers.

There is one period in an adolescent's life, especially with girls, when she acts like her mother is her worst enemy. While a part of the daughter's heart sincerely loves her mom, there is another part that seems to take delight in hurting her. It is a conflicted time of emotions and hormones that usually results in a rough period for both daughters and mothers.

These growing pains are not unlike the "terrible two's" when a toddler is learning to be independent. The child is smart enough now to understand much of what is going on, but not able to articulate enough to express his needs and wants properly. His dilemma of being caught between infancy and childhood brings out the very worst behavior. Similarly, a teen goes through frustrations, with sometimes very similar behavior, as they pass from childhood into adulthood.

The wise mother learns to become tough-skinned and love her daughter or son unconditionally. She must be an anchor of consistency, forgive and forget easily, and, as Hannah did, take her hurts, needs, and struggles to the Lord.

Always Keep Your Promises

*"Sir, do you remember me?" Hannah asked
him. "I am the woman who stood here
that time praying to the Lord! I asked him
to give me this child, and he has given me
my request; and now I am giving him to
the Lord for as long as he lives."*

*So she left him there at the Tabernacle
for the Lord to use.*

I Samuel 1:26, 27

*A*t the core of this amazing story is Hannah's
sacrifice and her willingness to follow
through with her promise to God. How easy it
would have been for her to rationalize a
change of heart. Lord, I know I promised to
give him up, but I think I need to wait a few
more years. He hasn't been feeling well. Lord,
he will still be a Nazarite, but he can serve you
just as well here in Ramah. Strong as she was,
Hannah must have at least entertained such
thoughts. But she realized how important it is
to always keep her promises, including the
private vows she made to the Lord.

As mothers, one of the most important virtues we can possess is that of reliability. We must be known as a woman who always keeps her word. To the best of our ability, we must do what we say we will do. Our family members and friends should consider us a rock of dependability. Though circumstances occasionally prevent the best-intentioned mother from following through on a promise, it should be the rare exception—not the rule. If we do not keep our promises to those around us, we will likely not keep our vows to God either.

What vows have you made to God? None, you say? Think again. If we consider ourselves Christians, we have trusted God for our salvation and, hopefully, committed our lives to him. We have accepted the Bible as God's inspired word and seek to obey its commands.

Our God is a covenant-making God. He has made many promises to us, and it is only logical that, in our very lifestyle and choices, we make covenants with Him. In accepting re-birth and redemption we have promised to live as Christ instructed us to live. Consider the following scriptures:

*Seek ye first the kingdom of God
and his righteousness…*

Are you putting Christ and His kingdom
before anything else in your life?

*Be anxious for nothing
but in everything by prayer and
supplication….*

Do you worry and fret about your children,
or relinquish them to God and trust Him for
their future well-being?

*I beseech you therefore, brethren by the
mercies of God, that you present your
bodies a living sacrifice…*

Have you dedicated your life to Christ so
fully that sacrifice (joyful, rewarding sacrifice)
has become a way of life? These considerations
are not intended to provoke guilt or feelings of
inadequacy, but to demonstrate that the
Christian life is intricately connected to
promises and covenants, whether spoken or
unspoken.

Our salvation is by faith, not works.
However, there are two important synonyms

for "commitment"; one is "promise", and the other is "vow." You just cannot separate the two. If you don't feel the need to carry out any obligations to God, it could reflect a low level of commitment.

Ask the Lord to show you the vows you need to fulfill and where you are missing the mark. He will lovingly help you to be the kind of mother who keeps her promises.

Studying the life of a woman like Hannah is valuable to us because we, too, can make decisions as mothers that can have a profound impact—on our families, our communities, and even our world.

We must never underestimate the potential that lies in a praying mother, who is thoroughly dedicated to God and willing to present her children as living sacrifices to this Lord whom she loves first and best.

End Notes

1 James M. Freeman, *Manners and Customs of the Bible*, Bridge-Logos, pp. 452, 453.

2 Thomas Cahill, *How the Irish Saved Civilization*, Anchor Books, pp. 138, 139.

3 Thomas Cahill, p. 141

Study Guide

More to Explore

*H*annah boldly asked God for a son and was not disappointed. Then she gave her precious son Samuel back to God. As a result, she learned the principle of receiving through giving.

God not only rewarded her with other children, he raised her first-born son to a position of leadership, where he had a profound impact on the history of an entire nation.

Read the following Scripture verses to learn more about God's promises and the power of prayer, then answer the accompanying questions.

- Matthew 21:21, 22
- Philippians 4:6, 7
- Jeremiah 31:16, 17
- Luke 6:38

Consider This . . .

What important need can you approach God with today?

_____

When your prayers are not answered quickly, do you give up or persevere as Hannah did?

_____

List some prayers God has answered and the length of time it took for the answer to come.

_____

List three sacrifices you have made to God that were difficult for you.

_____

In what ways did God bless you through those sacrifices?

_____

How have the sacrifices made by your own
parents affected your life? Your faith? Your
own giving to God and your children?

Was there a point in time when you
consciously prayed a prayer of relinquishment
to God for your children? Are you honestly
willing to give them up to God and his
purposes? If you have never prayed that
prayer, it is not too late. Do it now.

Wise Reflections

What does the word "sacrifice" mean to you? It may bring up visions of Jesus on the cross. If you are a parent you may remember delaying a vacation for braces or waving goodbye to a child who is leaving for the mission field. Perhaps you can't know firsthand the meaning of the word because you have never really had to sacrifice for anyone. Do you have what it takes?

Draw five boxes below and write the five most precious things in your life, in order of importance. Write the most precious of all in box one, the next most precious in box two, and so on.

Now begin with box five and ask yourself, "If God required this of me, could I give it up?" If you could, draw a heart in the box. If you could not readily sacrifice this for God, try to write down the reason. Then sincerely ask God to give you the courage and commitment to yield even those areas of your life to Him.

Remember the principle of receiving through giving and know that you will always come out ahead when you give to the Lord.

The Rewards of Sacrifice

*W*hen Hannah followed through with her promise and gave up Samuel to live in the temple with Eli, she had no guarantees she would ever have another child. Yet, God blessed her with three more sons and two daughters. It is interesting that we are not even given the names of Hannah's other children, Samuel's sisters and brothers. I have a feeling Hannah kept them close at home and kept a low profile. I surmise the experience of motherhood may have been more precious to Hannah than to the average mother, who might have less experience of sacrifice.

Over the years, Hannah was blessed not only with the children who followed Samuel, but also as she watched Samuel impact the nation of Israel in such a profound and positive way. One of the greatest joys of any mother is to see her child being used as an instrument in God's hands. The picture is sweeter still when she has dedicated that child to the Lord at an early age.

The rewards of a selfless, giving parent can be understood best by going back to the principal mentioned earlier of receiving through giving. Everything we give to our children comes back to us fifty times over. Everything we give to God is returned a hundred fold. We cannot out-give God. (See Luke 6:38.)

We could even be fortunate enough to receive the heady reward spoken of in reference to the super mom in Proverbs 31: Her children rise up and call her blessed.

Motherhood is a huge commitment for life, but it is an easy yoke and a light burden because of our love. Every sacrifice I have ever made for my children has been a privilege, and the only reward I've asked is to see them at peace with God, healthy, and happy.

The earthly love we feel for our children, though intense, pales in comparison to the perfect, eternal, unconditional love of Christ for His children. He made the greatest sacrifice for us. (Romans 5:8) Our God is our example of the ultimate sacrificing parent.

Mary of Magdala
Servant

"Sir," she said,
"If you have taken him away,
tell me where you have put him,
and I will go get him."

John 20:15

Mary of Magdala
Servant

My name is Mary. They call me Mary of Magdala because there are many women named Mary.

Magdala is my home, but it's been weeks now since we began our journey from the Galilee region to Jerusalem.

I had so many misgivings. We were all afraid to come. But Jesus insisted; we had to come to Jerusalem for the Passover.

Then, last week when we arrived, I thought my fears had been foolish. The way the people greeted Him, they loved Him—even worshipped him. As He rode through the streets on the little donkey, the crowds were wild with joy. They waved palm branches, sang, and danced. Has anyone ever received such a welcome?

The Lord's teachings and miracles those last days were greater than ever before, brilliant, inspiring and awesome! Our friend Lazarus had been dead for three days, but Jesus called him forth from the tomb!

Even with all the amazing wonders Jesus has done, we were not prepared for that. Even after the miraculous deliverance I experienced in my own life, I am still amazed at His power!

My heart felt as if it stood still as I listened to His words. And when he prayed for us, and for those who would come after, I thought I would burst with emotion and gratitude.

Then He talked of going away—and the heavy cloud of sorrow and dread settled down on me again. But never in my worst nightmares could I have imagined what this week has been like. The arrest, the travesty of a trial, His beating.

How could the same people who welcomed Jesus so warmly a week ago turn on Him and demand his death?

How could they spit in that dear face and strike him and mock him? How could they abuse so horribly this man who never did anything but good? Never have I experienced such anger and frustration at injustice. But I could do nothing, nothing.

Then came the crucifixion. The ghastly scenes play over and over in my memory until I think I will lose my mind. Thank God for the Sabbath. They had to end the nightmare and bury him.

I saw them lay Jesus in Joseph's tomb. I sat on that stone nearby until I thought I had turned to stone. Afterward, I gathered spices to embalm his precious body. It is the only thing I can do for the Lord now. Yesterday was the Sabbath, and I rested, but I have been up for hours waiting until it was light enough to see the way.

And here I am again. I don't even know why I came this morning. I will not be able to move the stone anyway. But I am drawn to this place.

What's this? The light is still dim, but it looks as though the stone has been moved! Yes, the dark cavity gapes at me from the hillside. What now? Haven't they done enough harm already? They won't even let the dead lie in peace!

(Narrative based on John 20: 1-16)

Mary Magdalene's Answers for Today

*M*ary was the last one to leave Jesus' burial place on Friday, and she returned there before anyone else that first day of the week.

When she saw the stone had been moved, she ran as fast as she could to tell Peter and John. They followed her to the tomb, but on discovering Jesus' body was gone, they returned to their homes. Everyone, that is, except Mary of Magdala.

What was it that drew her there? It was the same force that had compelled her to be there for Jesus and his disciples throughout His ministry. It was her love, devotion, and commitment to her Lord.

Even though she thought He was gone, she wanted to be near the last place she had seen His pitiful, broken, and bruised body. The disciples had given up. They thought it was over. But perhaps there still remained in Mary's heart a hope, however faint, that just maybe it wasn't over.

Mary stood there outside the tomb weeping. It was not at all unusual to see women gathered around a grave weeping in loud voices. That was customary in Jesus' day.[1] However, Mary was crying, not in grief at Jesus' death. She had cried an ocean of tears three days before. Now she was confused and frustrated. She was at a loss. What could have happened to Jesus' body? He had even been denied the dignity of a proper burial. Now she would not be able to perform this one last act of love, embalming His body.

Something caused Mary to stoop down and look again into the grave. To her utter amazement, she saw two angels in white sitting where Jesus' body had been. They asked her, "Woman, why are you weeping?"

Mary replied, "Because they have taken away my Lord, and I don't know where they have put Him."

She turned then and saw Jesus, but she didn't recognize him. Perhaps it was her tear-filled eyes that prevented her from recognizing this man with whom she had spent so many wonderful hours. Perhaps it was the early morning light shining behind him. Or perhaps Mary was still in shock and just not thinking clearly. But, for whatever reason, she thought Jesus was the gardener.

Jesus asked her why she was crying and who she was looking for. She replied, "Sir, if you have taken him away, tell me where you have put him, and I will go and get him." (John 20:15)

You have to love Mary's determination. She went to the tomb early that morning, not knowing how she would move the stone. Now she was resolute in her efforts to find Jesus' body. She never hesitated because, being a woman, she might not be able to move the stone or even His body if she found it. She intended to do what she had come to do, no matter what.

I'm sure Jesus looked Mary right in the eye and with that same strength and presence she knew so well, finally captured her attention. He uttered only one word—"Mary." Hearing her beloved friend and teacher call her name, as she had surely heard Him say it hundreds of times before, was enough. She knew then to whom she was speaking, and she bowed low before her master.

Who was Mary of Magdala, this obscure woman whose name and loving presence saturate the Gospels? She is mentioned fourteen times in all, eight of those times in connection with other women. But Mary of Magdala usually heads the list, and the times she is mentioned alone are related in some way to the death and resurrection of Christ.[2] One has to wonder why the other women did not return again to the tomb with Mary that morning. Perhaps they were hiding away like the disciples. But not Mary of Magdala.

Despite her frequently being mentioned in scripture, however, we have few details about her life. She was from the Galilee region, but her hometown is the only detail we have of her background. We certainly have no idea whether she were beautiful or plain in her appearance or how old she was, either. It is safe to assume that she was unmarried since she traveled regularly with Jesus, his disciples, and the other women in his inner circle. She did not appear to have any family connections.

One thing we can be fairly certain about is that this Mary was not the adulterous woman referred to in Luke 7. In that story, a woman followed Jesus into a respectable Jewish home, washed Jesus' feet with her tears, and dried them with her hair. Jesus did not call that woman by name, but he knew Mary of Magdala very well. (Luke 7:36)

Those who have made the assumption that Mary of Magdala was a prostitute or the adulterous woman who wept at Jesus' feet have done Mary a great injustice. Scriptural interpretations that assume Mary of Magdala was a harlot may be due to her having no obvious family connections and because she was from a large city, which had many prostitutes. But there is no scriptural or historic basis for this assumption.

The Roman Catholic Church is greatly responsible for this misconception due to its establishment of the first "Magdalen House" in 1324 for the rescue and care of fallen women. Great artists took advantage of this mistaken identity by turning out a generous supply of voluptuous, sensual women in paintings titled, "Mary Magdalene."[2]

One thing we do know about Mary's past is that she was a very different person before she met Jesus. In fact, this chapter might have been titled "The Transformed One."

One short statement in Luke 8:2,3 tells us that many of the women who traveled with

Jesus had been healed or delivered from demons. Mary Magdalene had been delivered of seven demons. Seven being the number of completeness may well imply that she was worse than the others—completely and utterly possessed.

What does a woman completely possessed of demons look like? How does she act? One thing is sure; it is not a pretty picture. Imagine a deranged, tormented soul, wandering the streets. Her clothes, what little there are of them, are soiled. Her hair is also dirty and tangled; her cheeks seem sunken and her, eyes wild and searching. Then suddenly those eyes stop their searching as they meet the eyes of total compassion. The evil, controlling forces within her being are banished forever with one touch of Jesus' hand.

What remains is a woman as different from the former creature as night is from day. What Mary Magdalene became after her encounter with the Lord is what entitles her to be included with the wisest and most outstanding women in the Bible and why I've chosen to include this study of her in this book.

She became a totally devoted follower of Christ. Her transformation was as complete as her need had been. She became a beautiful servant of the Lord.

I want to pause in our study of Mary for a moment to examine what I mean by "servant."

My passion for more than 25 years has been to help women succeed and be their best physically, emotionally, and spiritually. The very first chapter in my book *Growing Your Dreams* deals with self-image and how special and valuable each of us are in God's sight. Through scripture, I make a strong point for feeling good about ourselves and having the confidence to accomplish anything in life that God wants for us.

It is only after we realize our worth in Christ and feel comfortable with who we are that we can forget about ourselves and concentrate on others. The terms "servant" and "service" used here are positives, not negatives. They are synonymous with VIP's in God's sight.

With that in mind then, let us look more closely at Mary of Magdala.

Profile of a Servant

Let Jesus Transform Your Life

*And certain women, which had been healed
of evil spirits and infirmities,
Mary called Magdalene,
out of whom went seven devils…*

Luke 8:2 (KJV)

*W*e don't know what caused Mary to be possessed of demons, but the indication is that she came to Jesus along with other women who needed healing. They had, no doubt, seen the crowds that followed this popular teacher. Word spread quickly that this was not an ordinary man. Not only were his words magical, he performed miracles. He opened blind eyes and caused deaf ears to hear. Could it be that Jesus would heal them, too?

Mary's insanity was perhaps so complete that she had to be brought to Jesus by a friend. She might not have been aware of what was happening—until that moment when Jesus touched her and changed everything. After an encounter with Jesus, no one ever remains the same.

You are probably feeling pretty sorry for this poor woman, but also thinking you are nothing like her. "Oh, I may be needy," you may think. "But I'm not as bad off as any pitiful, deranged woman."

Most of us, it's true, are not insane or possessed of demons. However, we all need the transforming power of Christ in our lives. Mary was more fortunate than many of us, in a way, because her need was so blatant and devastating; it was undeniable. Our needs and deficiencies may be much more subtle, perhaps hidden and unknown even to ourselves.

As a result, we fail to seek Jesus and ask for his help because we feel pretty comfortable where we are. We may not realize that being possessed of sins such as ambition, greed, selfishness, materialism, jealousy, or self-sufficiency leave us as spiritually destitute as Mary's demonic possession left her. We may not realize it—or worse, we just don't want to change.

Before we can become a servant of Christ, we have to be made into servant material. True servanthood comes only with a personal encounter with Jesus. He is the only power that can transform us from selfish grabbers to generous givers.

You may not have the great needs in your life that Mary of Magdala had. You may not be possessed of demons or have a debilitating illness, or even be like the adulterous woman who so humbly washed Jesus' feet.

But we all need the touch of the Lord's transforming hands. That touch can take us in a single moment from spiritual ugliness to extreme beauty. The character, wisdom, and other virtues grow and develop over time, but the transformation that occurs from a touch from the Lord can be instantaneous.

Ask Jesus to reveal your true needs and then transform you, through faith in Christ's forgiveness, into a giver, a provider and a servant. (II Corinthians 5:17, I John 1:9)

Consider No Task Too Small; Be Willing To Do Whatever is Required

If any man serve me, let him follow me;

and where I am, there shall also my servant be: if any man serve me, him will my father honor.

John 12:26 NKJV

For, brethren…by love serve one another.
Galatians 5:13 NKJV

The first scripture refers to following and serving Christ. The second scripture talks about serving one another. They are both critical aspects of a life of service.

When Mary Magdalene was delivered of her satanic bondage, she became a faithful disciple. She literally followed Jesus and the disciples around the country. She served Jesus out of love, a hunger for his teachings, and the desire to be near him. She became, along with some other women, a vital part of his earthly ministry.

What does a servant's life look like?

What kinds of jobs come to mind?

We have already established that the term "servant" is not negative. It can represent important, intelligent, talented, even privileged people.

But, if we are honest, we think of a servant's job as the dirty work. Taking out the garbage, cleaning the toilets, waiting on someone else's needs. Those jobs have to be done by someone.

There are all sorts of servant positions needed in the kingdom of God. We may never be called on to clean the toilets though most of us, especially we women, have cleaned our share. But the important point here is for us to be willing to do anything the Lord asks of us.

I have often heard it said that someone has "the ministry of helps." I picture this as someone who is gifted with the ability to be at the right place at the right time and available to do whatever is needed. These dear helpers are far too few in our churches and ministries. They usually don't receive a lot of accolades or praise. Most people don't even realize they are around. Most never see the valuable function they have served totally behind the scenes.

Though these people are in the background, they are contributing to God's work in critical ways.

I believe Mary was willing to do anything. What sort of services did she perform for Jesus and his disciples? Have you ever wondered how Jesus and his disciples were able to travel from place to place continually without a home? For more than three years he ministered enroute, throughout the towns of the Galilee region, but also covered much of the country; He traveled to Jericho, Samaria, Nazareth, and, of course, Jerusalem.

The group of women, which included Mary Magdalene, traveled with the men or, may have gone on ahead of them, preparing the way. They had to secure lodging and food. Someone had to do laundry, repair the clothing, cook the meals, and probably help with crowd control.

It would not be surprising if this band of women also acted as the PR department. You know nothing spreads news like a group of excited women, and I'm sure these women did their part in getting the word out about Jesus' arrival, miracles, and the whereabouts of his speaking engagements. Jesus ministry could not have been as effective had it not been for these faithful women who worked quietly in the background, performing the menial, but necessary tasks.

Do you tend to seek the high-profile ministry?

Do you always want to be on stage, getting the glory and attention?

Or are you willing to do whatever job needs doing?

I am a bit uncomfortable asking these questions since I happen to be on stage a lot. In addition to speaking to women, I am on television every week in dozens of cities across the country. And I have often asked myself, "Is this really what God has called me to do, or do I just love it? Am I getting my reward each time I appear on TV or speak to a group of women? Will I still get a reward in heaven?

Those of us who work in "up-front" jobs need to be especially careful about our attitude of the heart. Though we may have to be intentional about it, we need to pursue a servant's attitude. We also need to be willing to step out of our leadership role from time to time and put on another mantle—the ministry of helps.

I try to make a point of working behind the scenes at church or at the office whenever I can. People are often surprised to see me cleaning the church kitchen or making the coffee. They should not be surprised. These jobs are in no way beneath me or beneath anyone else who calls herself or himself a servant of Christ.

The great thing about God's ecology is that he does usually call those who enjoy the limelight to more high-profile positions. Those who are not comfortable with attention are usually the ones you will find behind the scenes. However, we must be honest with ourselves when we ask, "Are we willing to do anything?"

There is not a more beautiful virtue than that of a servant's heart—a willingness to work hard for God's kingdom and for our brothers and sisters without seeking reward or recognition. Surely Mary's calling was the ministry of helps.

Be Generous With Your Time and Money

...Mary Magdalene, out of whom went seven devils, and Joanna, the wife of Chuza Herod's steward, and Susanna, and many others, which ministered unto Him of their substance.

Luke 8: 2B, 3

*W*e are all painfully aware that it is difficult to really do much without money. That sounds vulgarly materialistic, doesn't it? But it is a fact of life. Even in regards to God's work, money is necessary.

The same was true in Jesus' day. Jesus and his disciples needed money to carry on their ministry. We are told that Judas was in charge of the treasury. Where do you suppose the money came from? Luke tells us that Mary Magdalene and several of the other women gave of their own private means to support the Lord's work. Mary Magdalene apparently had personal wealth in spite of her earlier problem with demons. She willingly gave to the cause.

Generosity is one of the most attractive qualities for men or women. In a self-centered world that is concerned mostly about me, myself, and I, true generosity is rare.

My husband, Jerry, was once interviewing a seasoned veteran of ministry on a television program, and they were talking about revival. He asked this aging minister where revival began? To Jerry's surprise, the minister said without any hesitation, "Revival, my brother, starts in the pocketbook."

Jerry was taken aback and rather offended by this shallow answer.

"No, seriously, where does revival begin?" asked Jerry.

The blustery old fellow stuck firmly to his answer. He explained that when people's hearts are yielded to God enough for them to part with their money, God can do just about anything with their lives. I believe he was right on.

There is the well-known story of the trappers who learned they could catch monkeys by putting bits of food into jars. The opening of the jars were large enough for the monkey's hand to fit through, but once he grabbed the food in his fist, he could not get his hand back through the opening. The monkey preferred being captured to opening his fist and letting go of the food.

How often do we act like the monkeys? We grab everything we can, and possessions become so precious to us, we are unwilling to let go of them no matter what the cost. If we could only learn to open our hands, to hold loosely to the things we possess (they are gifts from God anyway), and to generously share with others; then we would truly be rich.

On the other hand, sometimes money is the easiest gift for us to give. It takes much more commitment and sacrifice to give of your time. Mary and many of Jesus' followers dropped everything, put their lives on hold, and followed Him around the country for three years. They were willing to give everything.

Tammy Maltby, one of my co-hosts on my TV program, and her family started the wonderful practice of adopting a family at Christmas. Her children had to take some of their money and purchase gifts for the needy children, which they were happy to do. However, when they had to go and deliver the gifts in person and become more involved in the other family's lives, they felt somewhat uncomfortable. Her son Samuel felt totally out of his element in the poor neighborhood and asked, "Mom, can't we just send them the money and not have to go and see them?"

True generosity takes time, commitment, and involvement, as well as money. But if we want to be a true servant, we must be a giver.

Paul tells us in 2 Corinthians 9: 7 that we should not give grudgingly or out of necessity, but give cheerfully. Wow! You mean, we not only have to give, but give cheerfully? Well, I'd say if you can't give with a joyful willing heart, give anyway. But if you want to milk it for the full blessing, give cheerfully.

The previous verse, 2 Corinthians 9:6 says if we sow sparingly, we will reap sparingly, but if we sow bountifully, we shall also reap bountifully.

Giving may not come naturally for us. It might be a little painful at first. But we can learn to be generous. And we will find that God always gives back much more than we give.

Keep Showing Up

*T*he most outstanding thing about Mary was that she was simply always there.

Her presence literally permeates the accounts of Jesus' life. The only other figures more consistent in Jesus' life were the disciples. Some have even claimed that Mary of Magdala was one of the twelve. A television program recently aired presenting that possibility.

I think the Bible is pretty clear on who the twelve disciples were, but it is interesting that even this program, which aired on secular television, recognized Mary's importance in Jesus' life and ministry.

The fact that Mary's name shows up so many times in the Gospels attests to her consistency and dependability. The fact that she was the last to leave the tomb after the burial and the first to arrive on resurrection day gives us a clear picture of the depth of her commitment.

When Jesus was preaching a sermon, she was there. When Jesus was being tried, Mary was watching. When He was being crucified, she was there weeping at the foot of the cross.

When He was buried in the tomb, Mary was there. And, of course, she was the first to experience the joy and wonder of the resurrection bcause she was there.

Undoubtedly, she joined the other believers on the day of Pentecost, receiving the power to continue Jesus' ministry.

Are we that devoted to God—or to each other? Can we be depended upon in hard times?

Mary's world had fallen apart with the death of Jesus, yet He was still first in her heart.

My husband has a motto that crawls across his computer as a screen saver. It simply says, "Honor God.... Work hard.... Keep showing up." It has been the philosophy of his life and the secret to his success. Always give God the glory. Be willing to work hard. And keep showing up.

Jerry has taught our children time and again the importance of work ethic, consistency, and dependability. I have often heard him say, "I didn't have a tremendous amount of talent or ability, but I kept showing up."

We all have days when we don't want to show up. There are times we want to stay in bed or go for a walk or do anything else but show up. Those are the days when our faithfulness and consistency are tested. Our true character is revealed by our willingness to be dependable, even when it's not easy.

Mary just kept showing up.

Rewards of a Servant

Mary and the other woman who went to the garden tomb with her were the first to discover the empty grave, but it was Mary alone that first knew beyond doubt of Christ's resurrection.

Peter and John probably felt as Mary had at first, that someone had stolen the body. But Mary Magdalene was privileged to be the first person Jesus spoke to in his glorified form. She was the first to begin to fully understand the extent and wonder of God's great plan of redemption. She was rewarded for her service and faithfulness in a way she could never have anticipated.

Even before resurrection day, I believe Mary's greatest reward was the time she spent with Jesus and the joy that came from serving Him. Mary, it appears, was a behind-the-scenes kind of person, who sought no public recognition. And I sincerely believe she was special to the Lord. He knew her heart, and appreciated the spirit and purity of her service. Jesus was not hung up on the inferiority of women, as was the norm for His day. He respected and valued the contribution of women, and Mary pleased Him especially.

What are the rewards of our service and devotion to God?

If we give of our time and money to His work or to each other, we are promised a whole cornucopia of blessings. I believe sometimes people live in want and need simply because they have not learned to be givers. Scriptures such as the one I mentioned earlier from I Corinthians promise a return on our investment of whatever we give.

When we are willing to do anything, are consistent, and keep showing up, we pass God's test. He knows then that He can depend on us. He will entrust us with more and more of His work. We will find that the fulfillment and joy of a life of purpose is directly proportional to the amount of service we are willing to give.

Again, this is not working for our salvation. It is simply a principle of God's Word that does not change: "Give and it shall be given unto you."

The more completely we give of ourselves to His service, the more blessings will appear in our lives. The blessings and rewards may not be monetary, but they will be richer and more satisfying than anything money can buy.

Someone sent me a quiz through the Internet recently entitled "Charles Schultz" Philosophy." Read through the questions and see how you do.

Name the five wealthiest people in the world.

_____

Name the last five Heisman trophy winners.

_____

Name the last five winners of the Miss America contest. _____

_____

Name ten people who have won the Nobel or
Pulitzer Prize. _____

_____

_____

Name the last half dozen Academy Award
winners for best actor. _____

_____

Name the last decade's worth of World Series
winners. _____

_____

How did you do? Probably not so well.
Most of us don't remember the headliners of
yesterday although these people are the very
best in their fields. There is not one second-rate
achiever in the whole group.

But the applause dies. Awards tarnish and
achievements are forgotten. See if you can do
better on the following quiz:

List a few teachers who aided your journey
through school.

_____

Name three friends who have helped you
through a difficult time.

_____

_____

Name five people who have taught you
something worthwhile.

_____

_____

Think of a few people who have made you feel
appreciated.

_____

Think of five people you enjoy spending time
with.

_____

_____

Name a half dozen heroes whose stories have inspired you.

———————————————————————

———————————————————————

The point is, people who truly make a difference in this world are necessarily the ones with the most credentials, the most money, or the most awards. They are the ones who care and give a piece of themselves to others. You may find it difficult to relate to many of the women in the Bible. The godliness and faith of Jesus' mother may seem far beyond you. It is perhaps too presumptuous to assume that you could show the same courage that Esther demonstrated, or the loyalty and self-sacrifice of Ruth.

But each of us can exhibit Mary of Magdala's spirit of service and of giving. We can, as women transformed by the power of Christ, be faithful and dependable and selfless. We can make an impact on this world by simply caring for and serving others. We can make the Lord and his work a priority in our lives. And we can keep showing up.

End Notes

1 James M. Freeman, *New Manners and Customs of the Bible*, Bridge-Logos, pp. 431, 432.

2 Herbert Lockyer, *All the Women of the Bible* Zondervan, p. 100

3. Lockyer, P. 100.

Study Guide

More to Explore

$\mathcal{M}$ary Magdalene served Christ in a manner that addressed His temporal, practical needs while He was on earth. We can serve Him today if we adopt the servant's spirit that Mary possessed.

We can bless and minister to our brothers and sisters. Christ said, "If you've done it to the least of these, you've done it unto me."

Read the following scripture verses to expand your study of becoming a servant of God and for others. Then answer the accompanying questions.

- Matthew 25:35-40
- 1 Corinthians 15:58
- Colossians 3:23, 24
- Ephesians 6:7, 8
- John 13:3-5
- Galatians 5:13

Consider This

What three things keep you from being willing to reach out to others or offer help on a regular basis?

How can faith in God's wisdom and will help you overcome obstacles to serving others?

Would you consider yourself an up-front person or a behind-the-scenes worker?

Are you using your shyness or lack of experience as an excuse for not serving?

What is the most difficult area of your life to yield to God? (time, money, marriage, etc.)

Wise Reflections

It's human nature to enjoy being served more than to serve. Isn't it good that Jesus didn't feel this same way? Neither did Mary of Magdala. She served our Lord with love and loyalty during his earthly life and even after his death and resurrection.

She was faithful and dependable; she kept showing up. It was not just a coincidence that she was at the right place at the right time that Easter morning. She was granted the unique privilege of meeting the risen Lord before anyone because she was a faithful and consistent servant.

Brainstorm for a few minutes to come up with five ways you can serve or offer help to others this week. Then list these plans in the column that is headed "Others." Be specific and include the name of the person or group you will serve and what you intend to do. Then, in the column headed, "God," write how serving this person or group also serves and honors God. Keep tabs on your progress throughout the week.

Others	**God**

Shunammite Woman
Hostess

"I am perfectly content."

2 Kings 4:13

Shunammite Woman
Hostess

*H*ow long has it been now? It seems like hours. When the prophet went up to my son, there was first silence; then I could hear the man of God pacing. I can still hear his muffled prayers.

What will I do if his prayers are not answered? How can I live without my precious child? I never asked God for a son. Oh, long ago in the first years of my marriage, I had hoped for a child. But my husband is so much older than I, and I soon realized it was not going to happen. That was all right. God gave me a peace and contentment that surprised even me. I am far better off than most of those around me. I have so many blessings—a good husband, a lovely home. Wouldn't I be greedy to expect more?

No, I never thought about children anymore—until that day Elisha told me I would conceive and bear a son.

Then my legs became like water, and I could hardly breathe. Had I misunderstood? I begged the prophet not to give me false hopes.

I tried to make him understand I expected nothing in return for my simple hospitality. Preparing the upper bedchamber for the prophet was a privilege for me. It has given me more pleasure than any of my so-called good deeds of the past.

Didn't he realize having him here with my husband and me, hearing his wise and inspired messages from God, were all the thanks I needed? Yet, he insisted he wanted to give me something in return. What an incredibly generous and unexpected gift he chose!

It happened just as he had said—one year later. Though I thought I was happy before, I could never have imagined the joy and purpose this little gift from God would bring into our home and our lives.

When they placed my baby boy in my arms and I looked into those eyes of innocence, and pressed that tiny body to mine, I knew nothing could ever compare. The hunger of my soul, which I didn't even realize I had, was finally satisfied.

Then, a few hours ago, when the servant brought my boy home to me pale, feverish, and so frighteningly still, I felt for the first time the cold and bitter hand of fear on my heart. As I sat and held my son and tried to cool his brow, I was so anxious for him that I felt as if my life was draining from my own body. I rocked him like I had when he was a baby. I sang to him and begged him to speak to his mother. And in my heart I cried out to God....

But my son died.

The son I had never expected or asked for and who had been such an unlooked for joy and a blessing was cruelly ripped from my arms. God seemed so far away. But his prophet was over on Mt. Carmel—less than a day's journey. So I went to him. It was all I knew to do. And he consented to help me. I knew if only he would come, everything would be all right. My son will live again. I know it! There, I hear the prophet calling for me now. "I'm coming!" Thank you, Elisha. Thank you, God.

(Narrative based on 2 Kings 4)

The ShunammiteWoman's Answers for Today

*T*his amazing woman knew beyond any doubt that her son would be restored. Her strong faith and her extraordinary life are an inspiration to every woman. The Shunammite woman offers us an example of so many imitable qualities—yet we don't even know her name!

Jeremiah the prophet is probably the writer of 2 Kings, which gives us the story of the Shunammite. Or it could have been written by one of his prophetic contemporaries.[1]

Regrettably, however, neither Elisha, the hero in this mother's story, nor the writer, bothered to give us this woman's name. Knowing her name would certainly would have added interest and a more personal touch to the account of her outstanding grace and wisdom.

I have admired this character of the Old Testament for years and was determined to devote a chapter to her in this book. But I hate the idea of referring to her again and again as "that woman" or even "the great woman of Shunam."

Please allow me to dignify her memory here by giving her a name. Often in her day a person was given a second name based on the city she lived in. Therefore, we can maintain scriptural consistency by calling our heroine Shunami. It's a rather regal and poetic name, and I believe it fits.

Her husband we'll call Simon (no particular reason) and since "ben" in Hebrew means "son of," we might have called their son ben Simon. But we'll just call him Ben.

Shunami's story takes place in a dark period of Jewish history. It's wedged in among the long parade of reigning monarchs of the divided kingdoms of Israel and Judah. Most of the kings were wicked with only a few decent ones thrown in and even fewer godly ones. However, in the end, the sin far overshadowed the righteousness, and both Jewish kingdoms wound up in captivity.[2]

Peppered throughout these books are the rays of godly light that were shed as prophets tried to bring Israel and Judah back to God. The author of Kings lists many of the miraculous acts of Elisha, and Shunami's story is obviously included because it contained some incredible miracles he performed. Yet, I believe Shunami is the real heroine of the story. She demonstrates a plethora of virtues that make her a woman of rare graciousness, the first virtue of which is genuine hospitality.

The Bible implies Shunami was a woman of considerable means, well known and respected by her neighbors. We discover a little later in the story that her husband, was quite a bit older than she. They were a happily married couple, and the fact that she consulted her husband in all matters indicates that Shunami was a submissive wife.

Their childlessness had not made them bitter. They had a peaceful home life and were in a position where they were able to reach out to others.

Though surrounded by idolaters, this couple worshiped the One True God. So they held genuine respect for God's prophet. Elisha was the only connection they had with God, and so he represented God to them.

As Shunami sat looking out her window at the road from Carmel (Samaria), she often saw weary travelers passing in front of her home.

There was something about Elisha's appearance, however, that caught her attention. Perhaps it was his manner of dress, or the leather scrolls he carried, or perhaps the way he wore his beard. Whatever the reason, Shunami perceived that this was a holy man, a prophet. (2 Kings 4:9)

She was especially interested in showing kindness to this servant of God. As Shunami reached out to bless Elisha, she did so with the purest of motives. She only wanted to serve and show kindness to someone she greatly admired. She was merely demonstrating her gift of hospitality. Never in her wildest dreams could she have imagined how this simple virtue would transform her life!

Let's look more closely at the gift of hospitality and at the word "hospitality." A modern definition is "the practice of welcoming guests or strangers with warmth and generosity." Hospitality comes from the word, "hospes," which means a guest or a host. From this word comes the names of institutions such as hospitals for the sick or hospices, inns for travelers, and even hotels.[3]

Hospitality is not the same as meeting someone at a restaurant and paying for her dinner. Hospitality is definitely linked with having guests in your home—whether your home is a single dormitory room or a mansion.

In modern times, especially in our affluent and busy Western culture, we scarcely have time to take care of our own families, much less practice the art of hospitality. Yet, it hospitality is not only required of us, it is a privilege, and it can be one of the most joyous and rewarding practices of Christian fellowship.

Anyone can be hospitable. And our Christian homes are powerful tools to reach out to a hurting world—even a hurting neighborhood. Here are some of the simple, but effective ways to become a successful hostess.

Profile of Hospitality
Start With the Basics

Now it happened one day that Elisha went to Shunem, where there was a notable woman, and she persuaded him to eat some food. So it was, as often as he passed by, he would turn in there to eat some food.

2 Kings 4:8

Shunami and Simon practiced the art of hospitality frequently, as did most middle eastern people. The Bible is full of examples: Abraham, Lot, Job, and New Testament families regularly had guests in their homes.

Only the very boorish would neglect to ask a traveler to stop for a meal or even an overnight. The traveler might be a stranger; yet the host would invite him in, wash his feet, offer him a meal and take care of his animals. The guest would be treated as a member of the family until he could be on his way again.[4]

Extending hospitality to one another is not an option for Christians. Though hospitality is not generally practiced in our country as it was in Jesus' day and as it still is practiced in the Middle East, we are given very specific instructions in 1 Peter 4:9 to "be hospitable to one another."

Perhaps the idea of entertaining or offering your home for hospitality is frightening or intimidating. You may not feel you are gifted in that area, or you may be so overwhelmed with bills, children, dirty dishes, and laundry, that you cannot even imagine having friends, much less strangers, into your messy home.

Given the demands faced by many women today, who are employed outside the home, such concerns are understandable, and there are definitely times when it's not convenient to have guests.

However, it is important to clearly differentiate between true hospitality and "entertaining." The words are often used interchangeably, but the meanings are different.

The dictionary definition for "entertaining" means to hold someone's attention or to amuse, as in putting on a show.[5] Therein lies the difference between entertaining and offering hospitality. Many are intimidated by the idea of "entertaining" because they do not have the money, the nice house, the fine china, or even the energy for "putting on a show."

The good news is that you don't have to. Anyone can offer basic hospitality. Starting with the basics does not mean throwing something together and getting by with minimal effort. On the contrary. The whole idea of hospitality is to make a guest in your home feel comfortable and special.

What is basic to you may take a lot more effort for someone else with lesser gifts, but the important thing is to always do your best with what you have to work with.

You don't have to have a large, fine home, or be a great cook. But you do have to first have a desire to serve others and, secondly, make up your mind to include hospitality into your schedule, otherwise it will never happen. You have to be deliberate about having guests in your home.

Start by sitting down with your husband (if you're married) and your children or your roommate to make sure they're okay with the idea. Then write some dates on your calendar. Or you may decide to have guests every Sunday or every other Sunday after church. Or you could choose one Friday a month, etc. You don't have to decide in advance who the guests will be or exactly what kind of gathering you will have, but hold the date. I simply write "guests over" on my calendar. Then I decide on the details as the date approaches.

My husband and I have been scheduling "guests over" days for years since we are both so busy. We try to lock in these days several months in advance. There are times, however, when we get really lax about scheduling hospitality dates. I am always amazed at how the months can fly by without having any guests in our home. It is a real loss for you and those you could be blessing if you don't make the effort to be deliberate about hospitality.

You may be thinking that your husband would never agree to it. Perhaps he's not a Christian and has totally different friends than you do. Well, again, think: back to basics. Consider having a neighbor over for coffee during the day or offering a jogger or walker a glass of lemonade. There is always some way of reaching out to others with your home.

Another aspect of basic hospitality that we sometimes neglect is how we treat our children's friends. We will often be quite willing to fuss over adults, but go to no extra trouble in making children feel special.

Sometimes the only Christian home a child is ever exposed to is yours. Make the most of pampering them, fussing over them, offering them special treats, or making them little gifts. It is one of the best ways of showing Christ's love to others.

My oldest son, Jeff, always had a friend or two. But Trevor, my second son, always ran with a pack. He would regularly show up with an entourage of eight or ten little boys. It would have been easy to shew them outside (and I often did), but I also enjoyed talking with them and feeding them whenever I could.

There were many times, especially in Trevor's teenage years, when I would awake in the morning to find long, lanky boys asleep on my floor, my sofa, and in my basement. I grew to love that. I developed a friendship with a few of those young men that has lasted through the years. I still feel like they are, in some ways, my boys.

A mother consistently has an opportunity to use her home as a ministry to other children, and she should take the responsibility seriously. Treat them to pizza (with their mother's permission) or ice cream or toasted marshmallows. You don't have to be a good cook to impress a child. Make a special occasion out of an ordinary one whenever you can. The memories will repay you richly for the effort.

Be Willing to Take Hospitality to a Higher Level

Please, let us make a small upper room
on the wall; and let us put a bed for him
there, and a table and a chair
and a lamp stand; so it will be,
whenever he comes to us,
he can turn in there."

2 Kings 4:10

Shunami had become very fond of Elisha over time, and one day she got a great idea! She decided they should create a small guest room upstairs and furnish it so Elisha would have a place to stay on extended visits. He would have a room of his own in which to pray, meditate, study, and rest. It would be a retreat of sorts.

I respect the fact that she did nothing without first discussing it with her husband.

But Simon enthusiastically agreed, and they began work on the prophet's chamber.

They were taking hospitality to the next level.

Though anyone can practice basic hospitality, most people can take the next step and get more creative and more committed.

This section will not contain recipes or ideas on how to set a prettier table. That is not particularly my gift.

I can have a decent sit-down dinner for 25 if I have to, but it's a big effort.

Thankfully, there are numerous books and magazines out there to help if you want advice on entertaining guests.

But my point here is to suggest that you stretch yourself and practice more radical hospitality whenever possible.

Radical hospitality, as we'll discuss, can take many forms. In Shunami's case, it meant building and furnishing a guest room for Elisha.

The prophet's chamber was a room literally built on the roof. The roofs of Near East homes were finished off with clay, which formed the floor of these upper rooms. The walls of the houses were extended upward above the roofline to form a parapet about three feet high. These short walls or sometimes railings were necessary for the protection of those on the roof. In Deuteronomy 22:8 God demanded the building of these parapets to keep people from falling off.

Upper rooms are mentioned frequently in the Bible. The disciples had the last supper in such a room. Jesus' followers hid out in fear in an upper room after the Ascension. These extra rooms could be rented out during festivals and holidays.[6]

Have you ever been reluctant to have an overnight guest because you didn't have a fancy guest room? Consider the simple furnishings of Elisha's home-away-from-home. Shunami provided a bed, a table, a chair, and a lamp. You may be thinking this was pretty minimal. However, it actually shows considerable attention to detail. He had a place to sleep, rest, and study.

Many homes didn't even have furnishings. The items placed in Elisha's room may have been very fine. For instance, you may think a stool seems rather crude. But the original word, "kisse" is the same word used in some passages to designate a throne. The chair and other furniture was probably the best that could be obtained.[7]

Again, it is important to do the very best you can for your guests, but don't compare yourself to those who have far better accommodations to offer. And don't feel guilty or refrain from having people stay over if the room you offer is not professionally decorated or if it shows years of wear. However, the guests should have their own room (even if it's normally used by your teenager), and should be given relative quiet and privacy.

You may be asked to take hospitality to a higher level and on a more frequent basis. Why not offer your home for a weekly Bible study? It can be a wonderful outreach to your neighbors. Consider having an exchange student stay in your home for a period of months. One of the most rewarding times my family ever enjoyed was to have a young man from Japan live in our home for a semester. He was a delight, and it was a great experience for all of us.

On the other hand, we once had a college intern working at our church stay in our home for the summer, and that was a horrible experience. The young man was lazy, messy, inconsiderate, and got involved in a questionable relationship with a woman at the church. Even worse, his departure date kept getting set back again and again until he had thoroughly worn out his welcome. It was a nightmare!

When we reach out with radical hospitality, we cannot always expect everything to go smoothly. But, in this case, we all learned from the experience, and we sincerely cared for the young man and tried our best to help him. Our hospitality with him was the right thing to do.

The time may come when you have to take into your home an ageing parent or a destitute friend. If you have practiced hospitality regularly, it will be easier to handle these unusual situations. And, the good part is, you have an even greater opportunity to use your home as a ministry.

Be Content With What You Have and Expect Nothing in Return

"Tell her we appreciate her kindness to us. Now ask her what we can do for her.

Does she want me to put in a good word for her to the king or to the General of the Army?"

"No," she replied, "I am perfectly content."
                     2 Kings 4:13 (TLB)

*O*ne day when Elisha was resting in his little roof-top room, he decided he wanted to do something in return for Shunami. After all, he was a powerful man. He was very close to the king and the leader of the army. He had his servant send for her. But when he asked what she wanted she said, "Nothing. I am content."

Here we gain more insight into the strong character of this great woman—she was content. How many of us can truly say that?

In regards to our homes and possessions, we often tend to be discontent. It's not because we are necessarily greedy, but it is our culture. Money, possessions, and status equal success in our society.

It's difficult not to compare our homes, cars, clothes, and toys with what others have. We often feel relative deprivation simply because no matter how many things we have, there will always be someone with more. The most unfortunate aspect of an attitude of dissatisfaction is we don't enjoy and use the blessings we have been given.

Regarding hospitality, the motivation and right attitude of the heart are very important. We must guard against "giving" to "receive." We should make a point of inviting guests to our homes that are of a different economic level, ethnic group, and even personality type than we are.

It is more comfortable for us to have guests with whom we are completely compatible, but here we must stretch ourselves to invite those who are different from us. It is also important to include on our guest list those who we know can never reciprocate.

One of the greatest joys Jerry and I experienced as a newly married couple was to invite recovering alcoholics from a rehab center over to our small home for Sunday dinner. Most of them had long since destroyed all family relationships and were completely alone.

One such gentleman, whose name was Cecil, joined us many times. It was somewhat of a challenge in preparing the meals since Cecil had no teeth. I tried to be sensitive to what I served for an entree, and he did just fine. We would talk and laugh and just relax together for hours.

Our home environment, which we completely took for granted, was a huge treat for Cecil and the others who knew only the cold, unwelcoming surroundings of an institution. We had many pleasant Sunday afternoons with these men, who could never have returned the favor. This is the best, most rewarding form of hospitality.

What you will usually find, however, is the more you reach out to others, the more they want to return the gesture. It is the simple Biblical principle of sowing and reaping, giving and receiving. (Galatians 6:7)

Though Shunami wanted nothing in return for her kindness to Elisha, he was determined to give her a blessing. He told her she would have a son the next year.

What an incredible and unexpected gift!

When she was building Elisha's little chamber on the roof, she could never have imagined her simple kindness would be rewarded in such a dramatic way. However, it happened just as the prophet said, and a year later her son was born.

Remember God Is Your Source

And the mother of the child said, "As the Lord lives, and as your soul lives, I will not leave you."

So he arose and followed her.

Now Gehazi went on ahead of them, and laid the staff on the face of the child; but there was neither voice nor hearing.

Therefore he went back to meet him, and told him, saying, "The child has not awakened."

2 Kings 4: 30, 31

Elisha's first miracle in this story was causing barren Shunami to give birth. The second miracle was soon to be required of the prophet. One day as the little boy went out to join his father in the fields, he became very ill. He was brought to his mother who held him gently in her arms until he died. What a cruel and unexpected turn of events. Shunami was devastated. She must have also been angry. She hadn't asked for a son in the first place, and now he had been taken away from her.

She knew what she must do. The man who had given her a son would also bring him back.

I am amazed at Shunami's great faith. She laid the little body in Elisha's bed, closed the door, and acted as though nothing was wrong.

She told her husband she was traveling to Carmel to see the prophet. This puzzled Simon because it wasn't a holy day, but he didn't argue with her. It's obvious Shunami was an independent woman whose opinion and wishes Simon respected.

This mother's actions in the face of dire tragedy teach some profound lessons for women today. Let's take a closer look at her remarkable behavior:

1. She did not panic when tragedy struck. She remained calm.

We say we are women of faith who believe in the power of God. Yet, when the least setback occurs we panic, or whine, or complain, or worry, and often make those around us miserable. Oh, for the quiet confidence of Shunami.

2. She did not spread the bad news. We sometimes take morbid pleasure in spreading bad news, gossip, and worse case scenarios. We tend to expect the worst and rally support

for our expectations. Shunami could have upset her husband and her whole household, but she remained silent. If she had blurted out that Ben was dead, she could have had scores of wailing mourners at her door. She wisely decided to keep it to herself.

Shunami and her servant journeyed to Carmel in record time. When Elisha saw her coming quite a distance away, he told his servant to go and see if everything was okay. He feared something might be wrong with Simon or Ben. But when the servant asked her she said, "All is well."

Here again we see her faith by her response. Her calm demeanor and positive greeting defies imagination, considering this was the darkest day of her life. She knew, though, if she could just get to Elisha, who represented God to her, everything would be all right.

The servant wasn't good enough. It had to be Elisha. Sure enough, when Gehazzi laid the prophet's staff on the child, nothing happened. Shunami wasn't surprised. She knew her source. She recognized the ineffectiveness of natural solutions. Of course, Shunami had done what she could for her son. But when she had come to the end of herself, she went to God through his prophet.

We should live so close to our Heavenly Father on a daily basis, that when emergencies come, we turn quickly and automatically to him for help and strength. We must grow our faith to the point where we can say, as Shunami did, "All is well."

There are times when fresh flowers and a good recipe book just aren't enough. You may find yourself practicing the most radical hospitality…caring for a terminally ill loved one or watching a parent with Alzheimer's slowly slip away a little more each day. Others can offer ideas and help, but it is God who is your source of strength.

Rewards of Hospitality

The rewards of hospitality are first and foremost the guests themselves. Elisha's company alone would have been payment enough for Shunami.

But, of course, she also received the ultimate gift, a precious son to erase the heartbreak of childlessness. An even greater miracle than his birth was his re-birth when the grateful prophet raised little Ben from the dead.

Shunami re-appears later in the 2 Kings, and we find that, once again, Elisha is coming to her rescue. When a severe famine hit the land of Israel, Elisha instructed Shunami to take her family to a distant place until the famine ended. Seven years later, Shunami returned to her homeland and went to the king to see if she could re-claim her house and her land.

In an amazing coincidence, Elisha's servant was just relating to the king the miracle Elisha had performed in raising Ben from the dead. At that very moment Shunami and Ben walked in! The king saw to it that all her land was returned; plus she was given the value of all the crops harvested in her absence. (2 Kings 8:1-6) All this because Shunami practiced the art of hospitality.

The benefits for us may not be measured in miracles or money, but the rewards of hospitality are countless. The best way for close, lasting friendships to grow is through the fellowship and bonding that happens when we share our homes.

Consider, too, the valuable lessons for our children when we open our homes to others. They learn to cook, to serve, to set a pretty table, to put others' needs first, and to be comfortable with strangers. They learn conversational skills and gracious manners.

Perhaps the greatest reward of all is the knowledge that we have provided a place of peace for someone who may normally live in chaos. That we have provided an oasis in a hostile and uncaring world. What greater reward than to know that perhaps in one small gesture of kindness to a stranger we may have entertained an angel without knowing it. (Hebrews 13:2)

It is clear the Shunammite can teach us far more than just how to practice hospitality. She was a woman of great faith in the midst of a faithless culture. She was confident, calm, and poised, even in extreme adversity. She accepted life's disappointments without bitterness. She was gracious, generous, and didn't mind taking hospitality to a higher level. She was a respectful and submissive wife. She served others with no thought for what she might receive in return. She was content with what she had, and she was a devoted mother.

I believe Shunami is one of the strongest role models we can find in the Bible or for that matter, in history. We may not know her real name, but she stands along side the other heroines of scripture with her head held high, her hand stretched out in welcome to her guests, and a serene and peaceful smile on her face. And from her smiling lips comes the declaration that speaks volumes of wisdom to us today.........all is well. "I am content."

End Notes

1 *The New Open Bible*, Introduction to 1 Kings, P. 388.

2 *The New Open Bible*, Introduction to 2 Kings, P. 426

3 Herbert Lockyer, *All the Women of the Bible*, p. 209

4 Arthur W. Klinck, Erich H. Kiehl, *Everyday Life in Bible Times* (3rd Edition), Concordia Publishing House, pp. 163, 164.

5 *The Concise Heritage Dictionary*, Houghton-Mifflin, p. 240

6 Arthur W. Klinck, Erich H. Kiehl, *Everyday Life in Bible Times*, Concordia Publishing Group, pp. 91, 92

7 James M. Freeman, *New Manners and Customs of the Bible*, Bridge-Logos , P. 172

Study Guide

More to Explore

The moving story of the Shunammite woman and her spirit of hospitality reminds us of the importance of having generous hearts and homes.

In addition, her story demonstrates the purest form of generosity—that which asks nothing in return.

What's more, on the darkest day of her life, she went directly to God (through Elisha) because she knew God was her source of help.

To discover more about how God desires us to demonstrate hospitality and a spirit of giving, read the following verses and answer the accompanying questions.

- 1 Peter 4:9
- Revelation 3:20
- James 14:2
- Matthew 25:35-40
- Hebrews 13:1, 2

Consider This

In what ways does having a hospitable heart help us to be welcome Jesus in our lives?

What are some qualities and attributes that help us be more hospitable to Jesus and to others?

In what way does Jesus offer us the promise of his own divine hospitality?

Does knowing Jesus is preparing a home for you affect the way you prepare your home for others?

Do we offer hospitality to others in hopes of receiving an invitation in return?

In what ways might you show hospitality to an angel without knowing it?

Wise Reflections

Shunami had a beautiful and giving heart. She offered God's prophet Elisha hospitality through her warm, comfortable home, and her selfless attitude.

What attitudes help you show hospitality? What hinders you? In the space below, write a brief paragraph describing one or more obstacles that might keep you from freely and joyfully offering hospitality.

Then earnestly ask God to deliver you from whatever it is that is keeping you from being the loving and gracious hostess he wants you to be.